Sumner County Tennessee

Bible, Family and Tombstone Records

WPA RECORDS

Heritage Books
2024

HERITAGE BOOKS
AN IMPRINT OF HERITAGE BOOKS, INC.

Books, CDs, and more—Worldwide

For our listing of thousands of titles see our website
at
www.HeritageBooks.com

A Facsimile Reprint
Published 2024 by
HERITAGE BOOKS, INC.
Publishing Division
5810 Ruatan Street
Berwyn Heights, MD 20740

Originally published
June 20, 1936

International Standard Book Number
Paperbound: 978-0-7884-8770-5

TENNESSEE

RECORDS OF SUMNER COUNTY

BIBLE, FAMILY & TOMBSTONE RECORDS

HISTORICAL RECORDS PROJECT
OFFICIAL PROJECT NO. 65-44-1499

COPIED UNDER WORKS PROGRESS ADMINISTRATION

MRS. JOHN TROTWOOD MOORE
STATE LIBRARIAN & ARCHIVIST, SPONSOR

MRS. ELIZABETH D. COPPEDGE
DIRECTOR OF WOMEN'S & PROFESSIONAL PROJECTS

MRS. PENELOPE JOHNSON ALLEN
STATE SUPERVISOR

MISS MATILDA A. PORTER
SUPERVISOR FOURTH DISTRICT

MRS. PAUL BARRY JONES
TYPIST

MRS. WALTER WITHERSPOON
MRS. ALICE GUTHRIE
MISS RUBY DILLON
COPYIST

JUNE 20, 1936

TABLE OF CONTENTS

BIBLE RECORDS

(TABLE OF CONTENTS, p. 2)

(TABLE OF CONTENTS, p. 5)

(TABLE OF CONTENTS, p. 6)

SUMNER COUNTY

BIBLE RECORDS

Copied from a Bible owned by Mrs. Eleanor Allen Sullivan.
Residence West Main St. Gallatin,Tennessee.
Copied by Mrs. Alice Guthrie.

William Trousdale Allen, was born June 14, 1853 in the county of Sumner, Gallatin,Tennessee. He was the son of Benjamine Franklin Allen.

Benjamine Franklin Allen, was born March 6, 1826. He was the son of John Allen.

Maria Louisa Trousdale, wife of Benjamine Franklin Allen, was born February 10,1828.

John Allen, was born February 24, 1776. He was the son of George Allen and Elizabeth Webster.

(2)

SUMNER COUNTY

BIBLE RECORDS

Copied from a Bible dated 1851 owned by Mrs Kate Miller.
East Main St. Gallatin, Tennessee.
Copied by Mrs Alice Guthrie.

Alexander Anderson married Phebe Hall May 30, 1787.

James Anderson married Elizabeth Nemo March 1815.

William Anderson married AsenathtMcCorkle June 1815.

Elizabeth Anderson married Samuel Wilson Sept. 7, 1820.

T.C.Anderson married R.A.McMurry June 6, 1834.

David B.Anderson married Laura Moore Sept. 5, 1871.

Alexander Anderson born Oct. 10, 1764.

Phebe Hall born May 17, 1762.

Elizabeth Anderson born Mar 30, 1788.

James Anderson born Oct. 9, 1789.

Miller Anderson born Sept 28, 1791.

Mebane Anderson born Aug. 25, 1795.

Mary Anderson born July 12, 1793.

Margaret Anderson born Jan 23, 1798.

John Anderson born Jan. 3, 1800.

Thomas Anderson born Oct. 21, 1801.

Jane Anderson born Mar. 5, 1804.

David McMurry born Feb. 1775.

Ann Blythe McMurry born Feb. 29, 1777.

James B McMurry born Jan 18, 1803.

John M McMurry born Sept. 30, 1804.

Elizabeth E.McMurry born Apr. 19, 1806.

Mary A McMurry born Aug. 22, 1808.

Rachael McMurry June 6. 1811.

(3)

David M Blythe born May 25,a1827.

Ann E.McMurry born Jan. 12, 1840.

Mitchell Donnell born Nov. 30, 1835.

Asenath Donnell born Aug. 25, 1841.

George Donnell born Nov. ___1844.

Amanda A Anderson born Nov. 1, 1836,

Alexander M Anderson born Nov. 23, 1838.

Phebe E.Anderson born Jan. 15, 1837.

David B.Anderson born July 19, 1842.

Mebena D Anderson May 12, 1845.

James M Anderson born Feb. 17, 1848.

Rev. Altexander Anderson died Feb. 1804.

Phebe Hall his wife_____ ____________

Mrs R.A.Anderson died Dec. 6, 1849.

Mebane Anderson _________1854.

Jimmie W Anderson_______ 1865.

Mitchel A Anderson died July 3, 1863.

Rev. T.C.Anderson died Feb. 3, 1882.

SUMNER COUNTY

BIBLE 1870.

Copied from a Bible owned by Mrs.W.P.Baker.
Residence 30 Hickory St. Gallatin,Tennessee.
Copied by Mrs Alice Guthrie.

Isaac W.Baker married Mary C Hines on the 24th, day of December 1839, in Bowling Green Ky.,by the Rev. Evans, witness by John L.Safferance & Gus Everheart.

Mary C.Hines born January 30, 1822.

Isaac W.Baker born January 23, 1817. The children of Mary Hines Baker and Isaac W Baker. 1st, Amanda Baker born January 13,1841.

2nd, W.P.Baker,born February 20,1843.

3rd, Hettie Baker born May 27th,1845.

4th, W.Scott Baker _______1847.

Hettie Baker died the 18th of April 1859. Age 13 years 10 months 17 days.

Isaac W Baker departed this life August 11, 1889.

Mary Hines Baker departed this life January 22, 1913.

5

SUMNER COUNTY

BIBLE RECORDS
1866

Copied from a Bible owned by Miss Ludie Bandy.
Residence Franklin St., Gallatin,Tennessee.
Copied by Mrs Alice Guthrie.

Harriett Pierce Bandy born Dec. 2, 1804.

William Pierce Bandy born July 4, 1823.

Elizabeth Ann Bandy born Apr. 20, 1825.

Edward H Bandy born Feb. 4, 1827.

Jonathan Bandy born Feb. 20, 1829.

Mary Samuella Bandy born Bov. 1, 1842.

Hezikiah Amandy Bandy born May 28, 1831.

Harriett J.Bandy born May 26, 1836.

Alex Epperson Bandy born Aug. 20, 1837.

Mary C Bandy born Apr. 3, 1839.

Samuel N Ross died May 19, 1858.

Susan H Sarver died Sept. 22, 1887.

Harriett Bandy died Aug. 26, 1831.

Edward H Bandy died May 12, 1850.

Epperson Bandy died June 6, 1863.

Capt. William Pierce Bandy died May 25, 1891.

Alex. Epperson Bandy died Jan. 1915.

SUMNER COUNTY

BIBLE RECORDS

Copied from a Bible dated 1879 owned by Mrs Charlie Whitesides.
Residence East Main St. Gallatin, Tennessee.
Copied by Mrs Alice Guthrie.

W.G.Barth born 1832, died 1868.

SUMNER COUNTY

BIBLE 1833.

Copied from a Bible owned by Mrs James W.Blackmore.
Residence West Main St. Gallatin,Tennessee
Copied by Mrs Alice Guthrie.

W.M.Blackmore was born the 7,day of Feburary A.D.1803.

Rachel J.Barry was born the 23,day of August A.D.1812.

David Blackmore, first son of W.N. & R.J.Blackmore born 25, February 1835, and died the 23, September 1856.

George Dillon Blackmore, second son of W.M.& R.J.Blackmore was born 24, December 1837, and died the 23,September 1839.

James W.Blackmore, third son of W.M.& R.J.Blackmore was born 9th, March A.D.1843.

Rachel J.Blackmore, died on the 14, of June A.D.1843 at ½ after 4 o'clock A.M. Suddenly of rupter of blood versal at the heart, age 30 years 9 months & 21 days. Funeral service by Rev. John Allerson. Text 24th Chapter & 44, 2 vers. Matthews.

General William M.Blackmore was injured by a fall from his horse on the 24th of November 1853 and died at his residence in Gallatin on Tuesday 28th, November 1853 at one o'clock.

Aunt Betsey died on the night of the 13th day of September 1865 at 10½ o'clock. "Blessed are they who die in the Lord."

BIBLE RECORDS

SUMNER COUNTY

Record from a Bible belonging to Mrs. Charles Bone, 3¼ miles West of Gallatin, Tenn.,Red River Road.
Copied By Mrs. Alice Guthrie, Gallatin, Tenn.
March 10, 1937.

BIRTHS:
William L. Bone,
Born Nov. 2, 1820.

Jane F. Clark,
Born Mar. 20, 1832.

William C. Bone,
Born Mar. 28, 1855.

Camilla Bone,
Born May 20, 1857.

Corinne Bone,
Born Oct. 10, 1861.

MARRIAGES:
William L. Bone &
Jane F. Clark, Married
June 18,A.D. 1854.

Robert L. Bone &
Sadie W.Russell, Married
Feb'y 14, 1884.

(9)

SUMNER COUNTY

BIBLE 1829.

Copied from a Bible owned by "The Brown Family."
Residence Franklin St. Gallatin,Tennessee.
Copied by Mrs Alice Guthrie

George T.Brown, born December 27th, 1807.

Amanda Brown, born January 6th, 1802.

T.L.Brown, born November 24th, 1811.

George T.Brown, born August 17th, 1837.

Susan Mildred, born July 27th 1839.

Charles H.Brown, born February 14, 1842.

John Crenshaw, born November 5th, 1819.

Amanda Katherine Brown, born April 5th, 1844.

C.Marcellas Brown, born January 8th, 1846.

Clifton Brown, born July 8th, 1846.

R.D.Brown, born June 20th, 1849.

Benjamine Brown, born July 25th, 1851.

George T.Brown & Amanda Brown married November 18th, 1830.

William Brown & Malvina Harris married December 23, 1856.

R.D.Brown died July 3rd, 1849.

Susan Brown died February 9th, 1855.

Mary F.Brown died July 12th, 1856.

Reubin Dabney Brown Sr. was born January 16th, 1777. Died in Sumner County July 3rd, 1849.

Lucy Thompson Brown born January 17th, 1784. Died September 2nd, 1869.

Reubin Babney Brown & Lucy Tompson Brown married in Alb. Co Dec 20, 1801.

Col. Bezellell Brown born July 29th, 1754. Died January 9th, 1829.

James M.Brown born November 8th, 1817.

F.C.Wilkes born Decmber 3rd, 1822.

SUMNER COUNTY

BIBLE 1870.

Copied from a Bible owned by W.F.Brown.
Residence East Main St. Gallatin,Tennessee.
Copied by Mrs Alice Guthrie.

John W.Brown of Gallatin,Tennessee & Minnie I Foster married Nov.26, 1872 by William M Green.

John Wilson Brown son of John and Annie Brown born May 17, 1848. Cincinnati Ohio.

Minnie Ida Foster daughter of John B & Susan born Mar.17, 1855. in Gallatin.

John Wilson Brown died Oct. 23, 1912.

SUMNER COUNTY

BIBLE MDCCCLXXV.

Copied from a Bible owned by Miss Annie Brown.
Residence North Water St. Gallatin, Tennessee.
Copied by Mrs Alice Guthrie.

W.H.Brown, born May 15th, 1846. Cincinnati Ohio.

Sarah C Hurmans, born September 28th 1847. Mitchellsville,Tennessee.

SUMNER COUNTY

BIBLE RECORDS

Copied from a Bible owned by Mrs Ellis Jones dated 1814.
Residence East Main St. Gallatin,Tennessee.
Copied by Mrs Alice Guthrie.

Henry Bryson & Hannah McMullen married Nov 18, 1828 by Rev. John T.Presly.

Edmond L.Patton & Mary Bryson married Oct. 18, 1859.

Hannah McMullen,daughter of Archibald & Mary McMullen born Feby 21,1809.

William Bryson born Nov. 4, 1829.

John Bryson born Apr. 3, 1831.

Little daughter born Apr. 20, 1833. Died Apr. 20, 1833.

Mary Bryson born March 21, 1834.

Robert Bryson born Aug 2, 1836. Died Sept. 21, 1837.

Jane Bryson born Sept 1, 1838. Died Oct. 12, 1874.

Sarah Bryson born July 1, 1841.

Henry Bryson born Jan.14, 1844.

Ann Bryson born June 5, 1848. Died Apr. 10, 1857.

Henry Knox Bryson born Dec. 19, 1851.

William Bryson son of H.Bryson died Jan.5, 1830.

Rev. Henry Bryson D.D.died sabbath night p o'clock Nov.8, 1874.

Hannah Bryson died May 21, 1886.

Rev. John H Bryson died Feb 1, 1892.

Solomon Wren died Feb. 2, 1829.

Lucretia Wren died Mar. 11, 1865. Born March 11, 1781.

William Wren born Aug. 7, 1801.

Abigal Wren born July 31, 1806.

Cinthia Wren born Dec.3, 1810.

Ann J Wren born May 19, 1813.

Mary J Wren born Mar. 20, 1816.

Louis Wren born Feb. 24, 1819.

Henerietta Booth born Dec. 10, 1798.

William G Hardy born Feb. 15, 1807.

William J Hardy born Dec. 19.

Lurertia J Hardy born May 29, 1836.

Polly A Hardy born Nov. 19, 1837.

Cintha Hardy born Apr. 29, 1840.

Frances L.Hardy born Apr. 21, 1842.

Martha Hardy born July 14, 1845.

Lydia Hardy born Feb. 15, 1855.

____Hardy born Mar. 4, 1853.

(14)

SUMNER COUNTY

BIBLE RECORDS

Bible belongs to Mr. T.A.Hogin
Residence 1 mile on Scottsville Pike, Gallatin, Tennessee.
Copied by Mrs. Walter Witherspoon
November 13, 1936.

This bible was brought from Ireland by the Carlen family.

Their 4th son, James Carlen was born 11, Oct. 1806.

Their 5th son, Isham was born 17, day of Jan. 1809.

Their 6th son Spencer was born 17, Jan. 1811.

Hugh ________Patsy Carlen was married the 13 day of May 1819.

William Carlen was born, 7th of May 1824.

William Carling the son of James and Pattasy Carling was born the 16 Oct.1795.

Their Daughter Sarah was born the 29th day of Apr. 1797.

Their second son Hugh Webb the 26th of Jan. 1799.

Their second daughter Hannah was born the 29th day of Apr. 1801.

Their third son Daniel was born the 6th day of May 1803.

Their third Daughter Elizabeth was born the 8th day of May 1804.

James Carlen was born the 9th day of October 1806.

Their son 5th/Isham was born the 17th day of Jan. 1811.

Sally Carlen Junior was born 30th day of Apr. 1814.

Francis Rogan was born Sept. 14th, 1778.

James Carlen died the 23 of Sept. 1813.

Their third son Daniel died the 26th day of June 1803.

James Carlen died Aug. 15, 1826.
Hannah Carlen died Oct. 22, 1827.
Ann Webb died Dec. 29th 1827.

Patsy Carlen Seignor dyed May 3rd 1848.

William Carlen Sunday June 18th this day 1826.

James Carlen 1826.

SUMNER COUNTY

BIBLE RECORDS

Copied from a Bible owned by Mr. C.K.Carlock.
Residence East Main St.Gallatin,Tennessee.
Copied by Mrs Alice Guthrie.

Job Carlock born Aug. 27, 1777.Died Feb. 2, 1855. Married Sarah McDonald.

Mary, born July 14, 1799.

Nancy born Mar. 10, 1801.

Susannah born Jan. 11, 1803.

Hannah born Sept 5, 1804.

Alicy, born Apr. 2, 1808.

Matilda, born May 12, 1810.

James born Feb. 28, 1812.

Benjamin born May 2, 1814.

Children by 2nd wife Elizabeth Johnson born May 19, 1794.

Analiza, born June 20, 1818.

William Baker born Apr. 5, 1820.

Jacob born Sept. 30, 1821.

Job Guthrie born Dec. 25, 1823.

Alexander Donnell born Oct. 16, 1825.

Isaac Newton born Jan 13, 1828.

John McSpadden born June 2, 1830.

Elizabeth Jane born July 7, 1832.

Lemuel Davis born May 26, 1834.

Job Guthrie Carlock born Dec. 25, 1823 died Nov. 22, 1861.

Children of Job Guthrie Carlock & Mary Elizabeth _____died 1927.

Martha, born Dec. 29, 1844.

William Baker born Feb. 12, 1848.

Columbus Kirk born Sept. 25, 1852.

Isaac Marioie died 1928.

Lacon Dillard,

Nancy Elvina,

Eliza Alice,

BIBLE * RECORDS

SUMNER COUNTY

Record from the Clark Family Bible.
Present Owner: Miss Corinne Bone, 3¼ miles West of Gallatin, Tennessee, Red River Road.
Copied by Mrs. Alice Guthrie, Gallatin, Tenn.
March 10, 1937.

William Saunders Fulton Clark,
Born January 7, 1806.

Emma Douglass Clark,
Born Aug. 21, 1810.

William Sanders Fulton Clark,
& Emma Douglass, Married
March 22, 1831.

Sophia W. Clark, Daughter of
Emma & W.S.F.Clark,
Born Nov. 20, 1847.

Elinor W. Clark, Daughter of
Emma & W.S.F.Clark,
Born Dec. 16, 1845.

Edward G. Clark, Son of
Emma & W.S.F.Clark,
Born April 28, 1844.

Reubin Douglass,
Born April 6, 1763.
Betsy Edwards Douglass (His wife)
Born June 25, 1774.

Reubin Douglass,
Died Aug. 21, 1832.

Betsy Douglass,
Died Feb. 9, 1839.

Peggy Green,
Died August, 1829.

David Fulton Clark,
Born July 16, 1842.

Reubin Douglass Clark, Son of
Emma & W.S.F.Clark,
Born Jan. 28, 1834.

Charles Clark, Son of
Emma & W.S.F.Clark,
Born May 18, 1839.

Elizabeth Edwards,
Born Oct. 2, 1840.

BIBLE - RECORDS

SUMNER COUNTY

Record from the Bible of William F. Clendening.
Present owner: Mrs. J. V. Johnson, 14 miles West of Gallatin, Tennessee, Long Hollow Pike. Address, Hendersonville, Tenn. R.# 1.
Copied by Mrs. Alice Guthrie, Gallatin, Tenn.
March 10, 1937.

William F. Clendening,
Born August 29, 1825.

Mary Ann Clendening,
Born March 31, 1828.

Robert H. Clendening,
Born Nov. 25, 1861.

Sarah Ann Elizabeth Clendening,
Born June 13, 1853.

S.B.NClendening,
Born June 16, 1855.

William R. Clendening,
Born Sept. 7, 1858.

Lew A. Clendening,
Born --- 23, 1861.

SUMNER COUNTY

BREVIARIUM ROMANOM PARS,VERNA
MDCCXXXIIII

Copied from a Bible owned by Miss Annie Brown.
Residence North Water St. Gallatin,Tennessee
Copied by mrs Alice Guthrie.

Cottage Bible 1771.

SUMNER COUNTY

BIBLE RECORDS.

Copied from a Bible belonging to Mr. Oscar Smith.
Residence North Water Street, Sumner County,
Gallatin, Tennessee.
Copied by Mrs. Alice Guthrie. November 16, 1936.

Richard Thomas Crenshaw, born Oct. 5,1820, died Oct. 25,1887.

Mary Fletcher Allen, born Jan.5,1830, died Apr. 24,1891.

George Thompson Brown, born Dec. 19,1807, died June 7,1883.

Amamda A.Brown, born Jan. 10,1809, died Mar. 5,1882.

George Kizzer Smith, born Oct. 4,1850.

Johnetta Luke Crenshaw, born Jan. 7,1854.

Benjamin Cornelias Brown, born July 25, 1851.

SUMNER COUNTY

BIBLE RECORDS

Marion B Custer & Mel J.Wilson married in Stewartsville Mo. Sept.15, 1870. by Rev. J.Parker.

Albert A.Delong & Mary L.Custer married at home of bride near Lithopolis Ohio, Oct. 2nd, A.D.1872 by Rev. G.W.Holderman.

Infants daughter & two sons departed this life July 3, 1851, Bloomtownship Fairfield Co. Ohio.

Monroe L.Custer died Feb. 17, 1853.

Emma Eliza Custer died Oct. 14, 1860.

Nancy Pauline Custer died Mar. 8, 1883.

Marian Ball Custer died Apr. 19, 1889.

George Ball Custer died Jan. 27, 1890.

Elizabeth Jan Custer died Nov. 30, 1901.

Nancy B Leach died March 12, 1850.

John C.Leach died Jan. 14, 1852.

Martha Ann Loyd Daughty died Sept. 16, 1832, in Frederic Co. Va.

Isaac Newton Leach died Jan. 20, 1845.

John Franklin Leach died Mafch 24, 1849.

William Thomas Leach died Jan 29, 1885.

Wilford G Leach died Oct. 10, 1887.

George Leach died June 16, 1894.

Alford Green Leach died Aug. 27, 1901.

SUMNER COUNTY

BIBLE RECORDS

Copied from a Bible owned by Miss Annie Brown.
Residence North Water St. Gallatin, Tennessee.
Copied by Mrs Alice Guthrie.

Henry Girard Dusenbury died 1904 age 51. Born Dec. 25, 1853.

SUMNER COUNTY

23

BIBLE 1833.

Copied from a Bible owned by Mrs Ellis Jones.
Residence East Main St. Gallatin,Tennessee.
Copied by Mrs Alice Guthrie.

Andrew Ellis & Mary Jane his wife were married January 9, 1840.

Thomas J Hay & Catherine T.Ellis October 31,1867.

Thomas Sherman born December 3, 1840.

Nancy Ann Ellis, born January 8th, 1842.

Sophia Jane born March 13, 1843.

Cintha Lucretice Ellis born July 12,1844.

Mary Lewis Ellis born November 17, 1846.

William Robert Ellis born March 29, 1848.

James Andrew Ellis born January 13, 1850.

Sarah Jane Ellis born June 11, 1851.

Luvenia Elizabeth Ellis born February 26, 1853.

John Baker Ellis born May 21, 1855.

Rebecca Ellis born November 14, 1790.

Johney Ellis born April __ 1793.

Robert Ellis born January 1798.

Nancy Ellis born ________1795.

Thomas S.Ellis___________1798.

Andrew J Ellis born August 1, 1803.

Thomas C Turner born Oct. 1823.

Wm B Turner May 15, 1824.

Andrew J Turner born May 5, 1826.

Mary Jane Ellis Mardh 20, 1816.

William Turner September 1778.

Charlie Woodson Ellis October 15,1857.

Deaths

Dianna Ellis May 19, 1840.

Wm B.Turner July 22, 1848.

Sopha Jane Ellis Sept. 15, 1848.

A.J.Turner May 26, 1852.

Robert Ellis Sr. Aug. 27, 1818.

Robt. Ellis Jr. Feb. ___1798.

Johney Ellis April ___ 1805.

Thos S Ellis March 10, 1820.

Henry Ellis July 3, 1824.

SUMNER COUNTY

BIBLE RECORDS

Copied from a 1854 Bible owned by Mrs Sarah Fitsgerald Lee.
Residence South Water St. Gallatin,Tennessee.
Copied by Mrs Alice Guthrie.

Henry Fitsgerald married Sarah William Bill at Memphis Tennessee 1850 by George W.Coons on the 23rd of July. Moved to Gallatin at close of Civil war.

Alice W Fitsgerald married Capt.J.B.Harrison May 1, 1872.

Sarah Fitsgerald married Andrew C.Lee 25th Dec. 1883.

Arthur Fitsgerald Married Annie Osborn Sept. 22, 1898.

Henry Fitsgerald born 22, Sept.1822 in Bandon Ireland.

Sarah W.Bill, born Oct. 1, 1831 in New York.

Alice Fitsgerald died 1892.

Henry Fitsgerald died 1864.

Emma Fitsgerald died 1857.

Rose Fitsgerald died 1861.

Lyman Fitsgerald died 1878.

Anna Fitsgerald died 1862.

Henry Fitsgerald died 1885.

Sarah Fitsgerald died 1922.

SUMNER COUNTY

BIBLE 1833.

Copied from a Bible owned by W.F.Brown.
Residence East Main St. Gallatin,Tennessee.
Copied by Mrs Alice Guthrie.

Minnie Ida Foster & J.W.Brown married Nov. 26, 1872.

Ellen Foster & G.A.Jones married Oct ___1874.

Elizabeth Foster & W.C.Blue married Jan. 8, 1885.

John H Foster & Florence Enloe married Jan. 7, 1889.

Rufus M Foster & Alice Turner married Oct. 17, 1893.

John B Foster & Susan Grinm married Oct. 14, 1834.

Susan Foster born July 20, 1813.

John B Foster born Oct. .2, 1810 in Va.

Ann Foster born Sept. 12, 1835.

Elizabeth Foster born Sept 14, 1837.

Mary Jane Foster born Sept 17, 1839.

Sally Mariah Foster born Mar. 22, 1842.

Susan Ellen Foster born Mar.24, 1844.

John Henry Foster born Oct. 20, 1846.

Charles Abram Foster born Feb. 7, 1849.

Rufus M Foster born July 4, 1851.

Winnie Ida Foster born Mar. 17, 1855.

Ann Foster died Aug 11, 1839.

Sally Mariah Foster died Jan 10, 1851.

Susan Foster died Jan 3, 1893.

John B Foster died Dec.1, 1893.

Rufus W Foster died Sept. 15, 1896.

Mary J Foster died Dec. 10, 1897.

Elizabeth Foster Blue died July 5, 1911.

Charles Abram Foster died Jan 18, 1918.

John Henry Foster died Mar 2, 1920.

Ellen Foster Jones died Nov. 16, 1930.

Minnie Foster Brown died Dec. 27,1932.

(28)

SUMNER COUNTY

BIBLE 1847.

Copied from a Bible owned by Mrs Emma Pierce.
Residence Hume St. Gallatin,Tennessee.
Copied by Mrs Alice Guthrie.

J.H.Franklin & Lucelia Douglass married Dec.18,1845.

Henry Franklin & Agusta Fuller married Jan. 18,1876.

George E Yeatman & Annette Franklin married Apr. 25, 1877.

B.H.Franklin & Eugenia Norris married Oct.13, 1874.

W.L.Franklin & Nanie Martin married Apr. 15, 1885.

Joshald H Franklin born Jan. 17, 1821

Lucelia Douglass born Nov. 21, 1822.

Annette Franklin born July 24, 1848.

Henry Franklin born June 5, 1850.

Howard Franklin born Dec 16, 1851.

Eoline Franklin born Dec. 15, 1853.

William Franklin born Dec. 31, 1855.

Isaac D Franklin born Nov. 10, 1857.

Joshua Franklin born March 18, 1860. Died May 5, 1860.

Emma Franklin born July 29, 1861.

Lizzie Franklin born Sept 15, 1863.

Minnie Franklin born Aug. 6, 1867.

Joshua Franklin died May 5, 1860.

Isaac Franklin died Oct. 29, 1890.

Henry Frabklin died Jan.19, 1899.

Lucelia Franklin died Aug.8, 1906.

James Douglass born Mar.15, 1702.Died Mar.21, 1752.

Eliza W Douglass born Apr. 24, 1799. Died Nov. 17, 1850.

SUMNER COUNTY

29

BIBLE 1885

Copied from a Bible owned by Mrs Nannie Frye.
Residence West Main St. Gallatin,Tennessee.
Copied by Mrs Alice Guthrie.

John Frye born July 20, 1849.

Nannie Frye born November 7th, 1850.

Nancy E.Parnell, born May 10th, 1811.

John Frye and Nannie E.Parnell married December 24, 1878.

SUMNER COUNTY

BIBLE RECORDS

Copied from a Bible dated 1831 owned by Mrs Walter Love.
Residence West Main St. Gallatin,Tennessee.
Copied by Mrs Alice Guthrie.

Cullen Bryant Gardner,"father of Mollie Gardner Herring" married Sallie L Franklin Jan 8, 1817.

John Martin Gardner married Selima Wynne.

James Franklin Gardner married Ann House.

Elizabeth Prudence Gardner married Dr Ben T Moody.

Mary Jane Gardner married Davie Grant Herring.

William Gardner born July 15, 1818 died 30th 1822.

John Gardner born May 9, 1821.

James Gardner born Oct.16, 1823. Died Sept. 12, 1826.

Isaac Gardner born Dec. 10, 1825. Died July 11, 1891.

Elizabeth Gardner born July 17, 1830.

Benjamin F Gardner born Mar.7 1832. Died July 12, 1834.

Mary J Gardner born Aug. 11, 1834.

James C Moody born July 22, 1848. Died May 23, 1916.

Benjamin F Moody born Sept. 10, 1856. Died Dec. 13, 1907.

Sally Gardner wife of Cullen Gardner died 18th, Oct. 1849.

Cullen Bryant Gardner died Jan. 20, 1865.

BIBLE - RECORDS

SUMNER COUNTY

Copied from the Bible belonging to Mr. Frank Gillespie, 6½ miles West of Gallatin, Tenn.,on Red River Road.
This Bible is dated 1855.
Copied by Mrs. Alice Guthrie, Gallatin, Tenn.
April 28, 1937.

Richard G. Gillespie,
& Susan C. Harris,Married
Oct. 26, 1853.

Richard Gillespie,
Born July 15, 1826.

Susan Caroline Gillespie,
Born ---1,- 1833.

George Marion Gillespie,
Born Dec. 3, 1854.

Bright Harris Gillespie,
Born Aug. 24, 1856.

Jacob Gillespie,
Born April 15, 1858.

SUMNER COUNTY

BIBLE RECORDS

Copied from a Bible dated 1853 owned by Mrs Susie G Gambill.
Residence North Water St. Gallatin,Tennessee
Copied by Mrs Alice Guthrie.

William A Gray & Sarah J Harris married May 23, 1856.

William A Gray born June 20, 1835. Died Feb. 19,1919.

Sarah J Harris born July 31,1837. Died Feb. 9,1879.

Catie Ann Gray born June 26,1859. Died Feb. 25,1930.

Charles William Gray born Sept. 10,1861.

Bright B.Harris born Jan.6, 1791. died April 28, 1867.

Sally Harris born March 6, 1794. Died Jan.6, 1863.

Abram Hassell born Nov. 17,1762. Died April 5, 1807.

Christian Spenwell born Aug. 1, 1768.

Pricilla Hassell born June 13, 1788.

Jennett Hassell born Nov. 16, 1789.

William King born March 12, 1783. Died Feb 19, 1814.

Pricilla King born Oct. 20, 1810.

Robt McKee King born July 30, 1812.

Wm Jennett David King born May 26, 1814.

Elizabeth Hassell born Aug. 30, 1830.

David Combs born Dec. 27,1773. Died June 8, 1844.

Christanna Hassell born Dec. 7,1809.

William Combs born June 27, 1806.

Salley Combs born Sept. 19, 1807.

Amelia Judd born April 24, 1810.

Penny, "The Great original" born June 13, 1788.

Fletcher, born March 12, 1830.

Mary Ann born March 18, 1840.

Polly born March 15, 1828.

Aaron born July 17, 1827.

James born July 7, 1825.

Noah, born July 4, 1816.

Jack born June 27, 1818.

Christanna Combs died______

Mary Howard died Sept. 9, 1818.

William King & Priscialla Hassell married Dec. 3, 1808.

David Combs & Christanna Hassell married Sept. 19, 1809.

Robt King & Amelia Judd married Dec. 31, 1840.

Abram King & Mary Howard married Apr. 14, 1836.

SUMNER COUNTY

BIBLE RECORDS

Copied from a Bible dated 1836 owned by Mrs Frank Dulin.
South Water St. Gallatin, Tennessee.
Copied by Mrs Alice Guthrie.

James Guthrie, born Mar. 28, 1779.Died Feby 26, 1840.

Elizabeth Guthrie born 18, 1780. Died Nov. 17,1859.

Nathan Guthrie born Aug 22, 1804. Died Jan. 23, 1832.

James Guthrie Jr. born May 27, 1806.

Mildred Guthrie born July 30, 1808. Died Feb.9, 1831.

Isaac N.Guthrie born Oct. 5, 1810.Died Dec. 20, 1896.

Julias G.Guthrie, born Oct. 7,1812. Died Jan. 31, 1861.

Thos. C.Guthrie born Feby 2, 1815.

Jephthah D Guthrie born Aug.21, 1818. Died Oct. 23, 1885.

Granville C.Guthrie born Aug. 21, 1818. Died Feb.16,1881.

William J Guthrie born May 22, 1824. Died Aug. 26, 1835.

Elizabeth Guthrie born Jan 22, 1826. Died Sept 7, 1855.

George W Beard born Aug. 12, 1823. Died Mar. 9, 1860.

David A Beard born Jan. 27, 1847.

Martha A Montgomery born Jan 20, 1827. Died July 30, 1877.

Elenor Heady Guthrie & Nathan Guthrie married June 15, 1813.

I.N.Guthrie & Mary Beachams married July 26, 1832.

Isaac N.Guthrie & Martha A Montgomery married May 8, 1845.

Isaac N.Guthrie & Margaret E.Taylor married March 25, 1879. Widow of B.D.Taylor and daughter of Thompson Hardin & Marjory L.Hardin.

Jas W.Guthrie & Mary E.Johnson Married Oct. 1856.

Nathan L.Guthrie & Adie M Gillespie married June 6, 1865.

Genry C Guthrie & Sallie L. Elkin married Oct. 20, 1866.

Isaac Y.Guthrie & Martha A Cage married Jan. 27, 1867.

Elizabeth Jane Guthrie & Jacob Livar married Dec. 20, 1870.

Emma Lettilia Guthrie & Legrand Scott married Feb. 28, 1872.

G.N.Guthrie & Ellen C.Hobson married Aug. 17,1875.

Frank C.Guthrie & Jennie Hardin married Dec. 17, 1886.

Mary B.Guthrie & Jim Whitesides married Dec. 12, 1900.

M.C.Guthrie born July 30, 1877.

I.N.Guthrie born Oct. 5, 1810. Died Dec. 20, 1895.

Margaret E Hardin born Apr. 13, 1832. Died Mar. 17, 1892.

Mary E.Taylor born Aug. 14, 1864. Died Dec. 4, 1879.

John C Levar born Dec. 25, 1871.

Elizabeth F.Guthrie Sept 23, 1833.

Jas.William Guthrie born Jan. 25,1836.

Isaac N.Guthrie born Mar 21, 1838.

Nathan Lewis Guthrie born July 22, 1840.

Henry Clay Guthrie born Dec. 14, 1842.

Nathan Lewis Guthrie born July 22, 1840.

SUMNER COUNTY

BIBLE RECORDS

Copied from a Bible dated 1850 owned by Mrs Frank Hunter.
Residence South Water St., Gallatin,Tennessee.
Copied by Mrs Alice Guthrie.

William L.Harper married Frances M Stratton Mar. 4, 1852.

Wm Harper oldest child of Jessie & Sally E.Harper born in Sumner county Tennessee May 13, 1827.

Francis M Stratton child of James & Joicy Stratton born Feb.6, 1828.

Francis M.Stratton born Feb. 6, 1828.

Victoria Pierce Harper born Jan. 8, 1854.

Isaac Summer Harper born Apr. 10, 1856.

Ella Beatrice Harper born Jan. 27, 1858.

Dora Athelia Harper born May 1, 1860.

Dr. Leauder Franklin Harper died Sept. 3, 1860.

Eacles Harper died Sept. 30, 1860.

SUMNER COUNTY

BIBLE RECORDS

Copied from a Bible dated 1850 owned by "The Lucus Family."
Residence West Main St. Gallatin, Tennessee.
Copied by Mrs Alice Guthrie.

Sylvanus Heermans & Hester E Lucus married 15th, December 1841 at Mrs M Lucus near Gallatin. Signed Rev. R Hatton.

Martha Lucus wife of Charles Lucus, born Aug. 20, 1792 in Culpepper Co. Va.

Charles Lucus born March 10, 1785 in Hallifax Co. Va. died May 9, 1839.

Sylvanus Heermans born July 15, 1817 Gallatin, Sumner Co, Tennessee.

Hester E Heermans born April 13, 1822 near Fountain Head, Sumner County.

John Charles Heermans Feb.22, 1843 Mitchellville, Tennessee.

Mary Louise Heermans born Dec. 10, 1844 in Mitchellville Tenn. Sumner Co.

Addison Heermans born Oct. 12, 1846 in Mitchellville Summer Co. died Oct. 14, 1846.

Sarah Katherine Heermans born Sept. 28, 1847 in Mitchellville Sumner County.

William Sylvanus Heermans born 19th, Nov. 1849 in Mitchellville Sumner County died Sept. 27, age 10 mo.

Madison Enfield born 28th, Sept. 1851 Mitchellsville Sumner County.

Martha Ann Heermans born Dec. 22, 1855 in Mitchellsville, Tenn.

Laura Francis Heermans born April 27, 1858.

Henry Clay Heermans born Aug. 11, 1860.

Benfield Madeline Heermans born Nov. 8, 1863.

Father of "Sylvanus Heermans" John Heermans born Jan.28, 1788 in Pa.

Sarah Heermans "Mother of Sylvanus Heermans" born Nov 9, 1799 in Rockingham county in North Carolina. Died June 1873.

Martha Lucus, mother of Hester E Heermans born Aug 20th, 1792 in Cullpepper Co. Va.

Charles Lucus father of Hester E. Heermans born March 10, 1786 in Hallifax county Va.

Hester Heermans died Nov 11, 1893. Gallatin, Tenn.

Van Ella Heermans born 22nd, Dec. 1855 in Mitchellville, Tennessee.

SUMNER COUNTY

BIBLE RECORDS

Copied from a Bible dated 1854 owned by Dick Harsh.
Residence Hartsville Pike, Gallatin,Tennessee.
Copied by Mrs Alice Guthrie.

J.L.Hibbitt & M.C.Martin married Dec. 20, 1854.

J.M.Hibbett & Loula Armstead married Oct. 28, 18__.

R.M.Gillespie & Mrs M.M.Hibbett married July 31, 1878.

J.J.Hibbitt & N.C.Parker married Jan. 1829.

Susan A Hibbitt & Wm McMurry married Oct. 1851.

Martha E.Hibbett & J.R.Franklin married 1856.

Mary E.Hibbett & Marcus DeWitt married Feb. 1860.

Vallie Hibbett & J.M.Pierce married May 31, 1864.

Andrew J.Hibbett & Mattie Philips married Feb. 1869.

Peter H.Martin & Jane Bell married July 2, 1818.

Mary J.Martin & Jno McMurry married Feb. 11, 1840.

Robert B Martin & N.P.Morgan married Sept. 5, 1849.

David B Martin & Susan Wiggins married July 11, 1859.

John J Hibbett Sr. born May 31, 1806.

Nancy C Hibbett born Oct. 30, 1808.

Susan A Hibbett born Apr. 15, 1830.

James Lafayette born Feb. 19,1832.

John B. Jr. born Apr. 23, 1834.

Martha Elenor Hibbett born Feb. 12, 1836.

Mary Elizabeth Hibbett born Dec. 28, 1839.

Valena Hibbett born Nov. 6, 1842.

Andrew Jackson born July 16, 1845.

Charlie Thomas Hibbett born Nov 6, 1851.

Robt. Melton Hibbett born 1847.

Peter Hinds Martin born Nov.4 1793.

J.L.Hibbett born Feb. 19, 1832.

M.L.Martin born July 22, 1834.

R.M.Gillespie born Sept. 17, 1827.

R.J.M.Gillespie born Aug. 23, 1879.

Peter H.Martin died July 26, 1849.

Jane B.Martin died Aug 15, 1860.

Mary Martin McMurry died May 2, 1845.

John C.Martin McMurry died Oct. 31, 1847.

John H.Martin died Feb. 24, 1846.

S.A.E.Martin died July 19, 1846.

Thos D Martin died Dec. 25, 1847.

Jas Hall Martin Apr. 19, 1849.

SUMNER COUNTY

BIBLE RECORDS

Copied from a Bible owned by Mrs Grace House.
Residence North Water St. Gallatin, Tennessee.
Copied by Mrs Alice Guthrie.

John H.M.Hillman born Sept. 27, 1841.

Thomas Tennessee Hillman son of Daniel & Anne Hillman born Feb. 2,1844.

Ann Fredonia Hillman born Oct. 19, 1847.

Grace Cora, daughter of Ann Hillman born July 16, 1858 in Trigg Co. Ky.

Daniel Hillman, son of Daniel & Grace Hillman born Feb.3, 1807.

Ann J.Marable, daughter of J.H.Marable & Ann born Feb. 17, 1818.

Daniel Hillman father of D.Hillman born Oct. 25, 1782. Died Oct.1831.

Grace Hillman wife of D.Hillman Sr born July 12, 1773. Died July 12,1821 age 53 yrs 4 mo. 10 days.

Daniel Hillman & Ann Marable married Apr. 16,1840.

John H.Marable & Mary W Jordon married Feb. 1842.

Evaline Smith & John H Marable married 1844.

Dr. J.D.Grant & Mary M.Marable married Jan 12, 1844.

Thos Y Dixon & Cora T.C.Marable married Jan 15, 1854.

J.H.Hillman & Sallie M Frazer married June 2, 1859.

Mary W Marable died Dec. 27, 1842.

John H.Marable Jr. died Apr. 4, 1844.

Ann J Marable died Jan. 26, 1860.

Mary M.M.Grant died Sept. 1854.

Cora T.C.Dixon died June 20, 1856.

Ann J Hillman died Apr 2, 1852.

Emily L.Gentry born Mar 17,1844.

Sallie M Frazer born Nov. 1849.

Dr. Edward Noel Franklin born Oct. 20, 1846.

Daniel Hillman born Oct. 25, 1782. Died Oct. 2, 1831. Married Grace Haines June 14, 1806.

SUMNER COUNTY

BIBLE RECORDS

Copied from a Bible owned by Mrs Harry Person. Bible dated 1831.
Residence South Water St. Gallatin,Tennessee.
Copied by Mrs Alice Guthrie.

Caleb Hitchcock & Betsy Gillmore married Oct. 30, 1804.

Caleb Hitchcock born Oct. 30, 1782.

Betsy Hitchcock born Aug. 26, 1785.

Dephia Marsh Hitchcock born May 3, 1810.

Kaleb Strong Hitchcock born Apr. 5, 1812.

George Hitchcock born Sept. 25, 1815.

James Hitchcock born Jan. 20, 1817.

Luke Hunter Hitchcock born Oct. 10, 1819.

Johnathan Hitchcock born Feb. 19, 1822.

Horace Hitchcock born Sept 19, 1824.

Sarah Jane Hitchcock born Nov. 19, 1826.

Charles Winchester born Sept. 19, 1829.

Delphia Marsh died Mar. 29, 1811.

Caleb Hitchcock died Sept. 1843.

Betsy Hitchcock died Sept. 29, 1845.

SUMNER COUNTY

BIBLE RECORDS

Copied from a Bible owned by Mr. W.L.Hunter.
Residence Winchester St. Gallatin,Tennessee.
Copied by Mrs Alice Guthrie.

W.F.Hunter married M.E.Roney Mar.10, 1872.

W.F.Hunter born Nov. 15, 1848.

Martha Roney born Apr. 24, 1851.

James M.Hunter born Mar. 8, 1823.

Elizabeth Hunter born July 29, 1822.

John Roney born Oct. 22, 1809.

Edna Roney, born Mar. 24, 1816.

Jas. M. Hunter died Feb. 4, 1885.

Elizabeth Hunter died Mar. 7, 1886.

Marcus Briley born Dec. 25, 1837.

S.M.Toliver born Dec. 31, 1832.

SUMNER COUNTY

BIBLE RECORDS

Copied from a Bible owned by Mr. L.N.Johnson
Residence 2 miles on Coles Ferry Pike south of Gallatin,Tennessee.
Copied by Mrs. Alice Guthrie. November 16, 1936.

A.L.Johnson, born May 4,1854.

Margaret Haile, born Mar. 14, 1854.

Susan Johnson, born Jan. 27,1831.

Ada Sue Johnson, born Aug. 12,1873.

W.S.Johnson, born Sept. 10,1831.

Julia A.Haile, born Mar. 16,1853.

(46)

SUMNER COUNTY

BIBLE RECORDS

Copied from a Bible dated MDCCCLXXIV, owned by Mrs George Glick.
East Main St. Gallatin,Tennessee.
Copied by Mrs Alice Guthrie.

John Craig Leach son of George & Nancy Leach born Sept. 17,1788, in Frederic County Va.

Nancy Boyd Daughty, daughter of Thomas and Elizabeth Daughty born Aug., 19 1800 Fred Co. Va.

John C Leach & Nancy Daughty married Jan. 21, 1817 in Va.

Wilford Gilkerson born Oct. 17, 1817.

William Thomas born May 8, 1820.

George Jackson born Oct. 2, 1822.

Elizabeth Jane born May 6, 1825.

John Franklin born Sept. 14, 1827.

Martha Ann Loyd Daughty born Mar 7, 1830.

Eliza Ann born Aug. 13, 1832.

Alfred Green born Dec. 15, 1834.

Maryanne born May 9, 1839.

Isaac Newton born Dec. 27,1841.

Gen. George B Custer son of George & Mary Custer born Aug. 16, 1810.In Washington Co. Penn.

Marion B Custer born Nov. 24, 1848. Infants a daughter & two sons July 3, 1851.

Monroe L Custer born Aug. 27, 1854 (corrected by hand to 1852). Fairfield Co. Ohio.

Mary Laurene Custer born July 14, 1854.

Nancy Pauline Custer born Oct. 24, 1856.

Emma Eliza Custer born Sept 15, 1860.

George B Custer & Elizabeth Jane Leach married Feb. 8, 1848 by Rev. Samuel Wilson.

(47)

SUMNER COUNTY

BIBLE RECORDS

Copied from a Bible dated 1834 owned by Misses Love Kate & Sally.
Residence North Water St., Gallatin, Tennessee.
Copied by Mrs Alice Guthrie.

James F.Love married Mariah Elliott Jan 8, 1835.

James F.Love & Malinda Elliott married Nov 17, 1842.

George Love born Oct. 18, 1855.

Iva Ann Love born Sept 7, 1837.

Hugh E.Love born June 24, 1840.

Mariah E.Love born Jan 12, 1842.

S.W.Love born Aug. 20, 1845.

Margaret Matilda Love born Nov. 1, 1850.

Richard Love born Sept 27, 1847.

James F.Love born Feb. 10, 1852. Died Apr. 10, 1910.

Slaves Birth

Jake, May 10, 1846.	Mary Nov. 23, 1848.
Louisa May 15, 1850.	Peter, Dec.23, 1851.

Sarah Ann Elliott born Nov. 23, 1839.

Elenor I Elliott, born Nov. 23, 1841.

Simon Elliott born Aug. 14, 1842.

William Soloman Elliott, born Oct. 31, 1844.

James Elliott, born May 27, 1846.

Margaret Elliott Mar. 22, 1848.

Julias Elliott born June 20, 1849.

James Hixon born Dec. 4, 1841.

Maggie Ela born Mar. 15, 1865.

Mariah Love died Jan. 14, 1842.

Jefferson Love died July 4, 1844.

James F.Love died Sept. 26, 1852.

48

Malinda Love died Oct. 30, 1853.

Ivy Love died Mar. 14, 1859.

George Love died Apr. 11, 1864.

Mollie Hixon died Apr. 12, 1868.

Charles Hixon died Apr. 17, 1879.

Richard Hixon died Feb. 9, 1873.

Lula Hixon died Feb. 21, 1875.

Polly Love born Oct. 30, 1794.

Betsy Love born Dec. 3, 1797.

Wiliam Love born Feb. 25, 1801.

Marget Love born Feb. 11, 1807.

George Love born June 8, 1805.

James F.Love born Jan. 5,1810.

Hiram Love born Jan. 16, 1812.

Thomas I.Love born July 14, 1813.

Delila Love born July 22, 1815.

Delany Love born Apr. 22, 1817.

Lousa Love born Jan. 1, 1819.

Soloman Love born Mar. 11, 1820.

Jane Love born Oct. 4, 1821.

SUMNER COUNTY

BIBLE RECORDS

Copied from a Bible dated 1854 owned by "The Lucus Family."
Residence West Main St. Gallatin,Tennessee
Copied by Mrs Alice Guthrie.

Mat J Lucus born Feby, 28, 1828.

Martha D Lucus wife of Mat J Lucus born April 17, 1840.

Mat J Lucus & Martha D Trigg married Oct. 9, 1856 in Gallatin, Tennessee.

SUMNER COUNTY

BIBLE RECORDS

Copied from a Bible dated 1820 owned by Mrs Nancy Timberman.
Residence South Water St. Gallatin,Tennessee.
Copied by Mrs Alice Guthrie.

Peter H Martin Born Nov. 4, 1793.

Jane Bell Martin born July 24, 1795.

Mary Jane Martin born June 21, 1899.

John Henley Martin born Jan.6, 1821.

Thos Duncan born June 2, 1822.

Sarah Ann Elizabeth Martin born Nov. 4, 1823.

Peter Hinds Martin born June 5, 1825.

Robt Bell Martin born Apr. 1, 1827.

James Hall Martin born Feb. 5, 1829.

David Bell Martin born Dec. 28, 1830.

Joseph D.Martin born Sept 22, 1832.

Martha Cathrine Martin born July 22, 1834.

Matilda Louisa Martin born May 31, 1836.

Gidean Blackman born Aug. 23, 1840.

Peter Hinds Martin married Jane Bell July 2, 1818.

Mary Jane Martin married John C McMurray Feb. 11, 1841.

Jane Martin died Aug. 1, 1860.

Peter Hinds Martin & Jane Bell Martin joined the church on earth of our Lord & Savior A.D.Aug 31, 1828 in the town of Gallatin, Tennessee.

Mary Martin McMurry died 1845 age 25, May 15th.

Peter H Martin died July 20, 1849.

SUMNER COUNTY

BIBLE RECORDS

Copied from a Bible owned by Misses Love, Kate & Sally.
Residence North Water St. Gallatin,Tennessee.
Copied by Mrs Alice Guthrie.

John F McMurry born June 11, 1825.

Sarah Allan McMurry born Nov. 30, 1825. married Dec. 14, 1848.

Sopha B McMurry born Sept 24, 1849.

Martha Ann McMurry born May 13, 1851.

Mary Elizabeth McMurry born June 19, 1853.

Samuel Houston McMurry born July 3, 1855.

George Etta McMurry born Aug. 20, 1860.

BIBLE - RECORDS

SUMNER COUNTY

Record from the Mitchell Family Bible.
Present owner: Mrs. Mary Ann Mitchell.
Residence: 9½ miles West of Gallatin,Tenn.,on the Station Camp Creek Road.
Copied by Mrs. Alice Guthrie, Gallatin, Tennessee.
April 12, 1937.

W. J. Mitchell &
Mary Ann Jones,
Married March 12, 1882.

V. J. Mitchell &
Clara B. Cummings,
Married Dec. 25, 1910.

SUMNER COUNTY

BIBLE RECORDS

Copied from a Bible dated 1843 owned by Miss Anderson.
Residence East Main St.Gallatin,Tennessee.
Copied by Mrs Alice Guthrie.

William Moore married Catherine C Howell Dec.19, 1844.

Theo Frieberg married Lelia A Moore Feb. 18, 1886.

George Elliott Moore born Sept. 19, 184?.

Catherine Ann Moore born Sept. 5, 1847.

John Thos Moore born Mar.1, 1848.

William Jesse Moore born Nov. 26, 1850.

Lilia A Moore born July 31, 1856.

Elisebeth Moore born Aug. 23, 1854.

Benetta Moore born Dec. 13, 1858.

Kate Moore born Nov. 14, 1864.

SUMNER COUNTY

BIBLE RECORDS

Copied from a Bible dated 1856 owned by Mrs Robert Morris.
Residence Smith St. Gallatin, Tennessee.
Copied by Mrs Alice Guthrie.

Robert Morris Jr. born Dec. 11, 1849.

Eliza La Rue Blakey born Jan 31, 1853.

Robt Morris died July 31, 1888 age 70 years.

Robert Morris Jr. died Dec. 25, 1928.

BIBLE - RECORDS

SUMNER COUNTY

Record from the Bible of J. D. Nesbitt.
Present owner: Mrs. O. W. Cozzort, 15 miles West of Gallatin Tenn.,on Long Hollow Pike; address,Hendersonville, Tenn.R.# 1. (Mrs. Cozzort formerly lived in Columbia, Tenn.)
Copied by Mrs. Alice Guthrie, Gallatin, Tenn.
March 10, 1937.

J. D. Nesbitt,
Born Dec. 23, 1824.

Martha Macon Nesbitt,
Born April 3, 1823.

Elizabeth J. Nesbitt,
Born July 25, 1845.

William J. Nesbitt,
Born Sept. 5, 1847.

J. M. A. Nesbitt,
Born Dec. 13, 1849.

Nancy O.K.Moore Nesbitt,
Born March 5, 1857.

Eliza Helen Nesbitt,
Born March 29, 1859.

Mattie Warren Nesbitt,
Born Nov. 15, 1861.

Allice Granger Nesbitt,
Born Sept. 24, 1864.

Martha Macon Nesbitt,
Died Sept. 24, 1864.

Allice Granger Nesbitt,
Died Feb. 5, 1865.

SUMNER COUNTY

BIBLE RECORDS

Copied from a Bible owned by Misses Peyton.
Residence West Main St. Gallatin, Tennessee.
Copied by Mrs Alice Guthrie.

Margaret Peyton died 1812.

John Peyton Sr. Aug 20, 1833.

Margaret Barry died Aug 21, 1834.

William R Peyton died July 20, 1846.

Ann C Peyton died Jan 14, 1845.

Joseph H Peyton died Nov 11, 1845.

Emely Turner Peyton born April 8, 1831.

Balie Peyton born Apr. 23, 1833.

John Bell Peyton born Feb. 13, 1836.

Ann C Peyton born Sept 17, 1840.

Joseph H Peyton & Mary Elizabeth Hatton married April 6, 1841.

Rebecca H Peyton & George W Parker married May 18, 1830.

Balie Peyton & Ann C Smith married May 20, 1830.

John Peyton & Mary Hamilton married Dec. 25, 1790.

Sarah H Peyton & Thomas Barry married Nov. 16, 1830.

Joseph H Peyton & Mary E Hatton married Apr. 6, 1841.

John Campbell Peyton born Feb. 7, 1842.

Joseph Balie Peyton born May 15, 1845.

Redmond Barry born Dec. 1, 1831.

Margaret Barry born Feb. 15, 1834.

John C Hamilton born May 5, 1774.

Joseph H Peyton born May 20, 1839.

SUMNER COUNTY

BIBLE 1859.

Copied from a Bible owned by Miss Annie Brown.
Residence North Water St. Gallatin,Tennessee
Copied by Mrs Alice Guthrie.

Ann J.Reilly & Charles H.Reed married Oct. 15th, 1858. Memphis,Tennessee.

Ann J.Reilly born July 23rd, 1844 in the villiage of Kings court County Cavaron Ireland.

Charles Harford Reed born March 8th, 1830 New Yonk City, N.Y.

SUMNER COUNTY

BIBLE RECORDS

Copied from a bible belonging to Mr Claude Senter.
Residence in Bethpage Tennessee 10 miles east of Gallatin on Scottsville Pike, Gallatin, Tennessee.
Copied by Mrs. Alice Guthrie - Date November 13, 1936/

John Thomas Senter, born May 24,1847, died Nov.5,1889.

Martha Alexander Key, born Nov.10,1853, died Mar. 8,1917.

Martha Alexander Key & John Thomas Senter-Married Nov.16,1871.

SUMNER COUNTY

BIBLE 1850

Copied from a Bible owned by Miss Nell Houston Brown.
Residence East Main St. Gallatin,Tennessee
Copied by Mrs Alice Guthrie.

William Houston Soloman & Elizabeth Boyers married Dec. 20,1853 by Rev. W.H.Hunsen.

Willie Houston Soloman, daughter of Elizabeth & William H.Soloman married Chas B.Brown Nov. 6,1883.

2nd marriage of Elizabeth Soloman to Cincinnatus W Boyers dec. 20,1870.

Willie Houston daughter of William H and Elizabeth Soloman born Mar.14, 1860.

W.H.Soloman died April 18,1860.

Willie Houston Brown died Jan. 27,1886.

Elizabeth Soloman Boyers died Nov. 18,1901.

Mary E.Soloman infant died Jan. 23,1859.

Thomas Boyers & Annie O Mahoney Brown married Oct.13,1852.

Robert, son of Thomas and Annie Boyers born Aug.4, 1853.

Cincinnatus Boyers died Apr. 21,1881.

SUMNER COUNTY

BIBLE RECORDS

Copied from a Bible owned by Miss Anna Lou Neal.
Residence Franklin St. Gallatin,Tennessee.
Copied by Mrs Alice Guthrie.

Col. Lyttleton Spivey married Celia Nazareth Cowart Oct. 1804.

Celia N.Spevey married Avner Burnham.

John Madison Chastain & Sophia Elmina Spivy married Oct. 1836.

James A Spivey married Anna Hangaboot 1848.

Clifford Burnham married John Davis 1863.

William A Houser married Francis Celia Chastain Feb. 2, 1858.

Sophia Elmina born Sept. 9, 1822.

Leonidas Chastain born Jan. 30, 1859.

SUMNER COUNTY

BIBLE RECORDS

Copied from a Bible dated 1835 owned by Mrs John R Harris.
Residence East Main St. Gallatin,Tennessee.
Copied by Mrs Alice Guthrie.

Thomas Surber born Aug. 25, 1807.

Maria Evans born Jan.4, 1812.

Galm E Surber born Jan. 18, 1829. Died Nov. 28, 1850.

Jeremiah Surber born Feb. 10, 1830. Died Jan. 28, 1869.

Harriett Surber born July 26, 1832.

Nancy Jane Surber born Oct. 23, 1834.

Margret Surber born Feb. 15, 1837.

Sarah Surber born Jan. 16, 1840.

Martha Ann Surber born Sept. 29, 1842.

William S.E.Surber born May 15, 1845.

John Purkins Surber born Jan. 30, 1848.

Thomas Caldwell born Sept. 27, 1850.

Henry Latin Surber born May 28, 1853.

Daniel Fox Surber born May 25, 1858.

Henry Surber born Nov. 14, 1777.

Sariah Surber born Oct. 12, 1780.

Grim Surber born Jan. 22, 1854.

Maria Surber died March 12, 1872.

Sarah Surber & Volney Barker married June 26, 1855.

Harriett S Surber & William Hudson married April 13, 1853.

Thomas Surber & Maria Surber married March 9, 1828.

Martha A Surber & Wm Y Taylor married Dec. 20, 1864.

John P Surber & Francis C Stewart married Jan. 12, 1868.

SUMNER COUNTY

BIBLE RECORDS

Copied from a Bible dated 1810 owned by Robert Sindle.
Residence Bledsoe St. Gallatin,Tennessee.
Copied by Mrs Alice Guthrie.

Eliza Ann Swartezwelder was born the 13th day of May 1818.

Mary Elener Swartezwelder was born the 8th, day of Oct. 1820.

Martha Jane was born the 4th, of May 1823.

John Westley Swartezwelder was born the 6th, day of April 1824.

John Westley Swarte/zwelder departed this life Dec. 20, 1829.

Mary Ellen was married the 13th, ____1842.

Cynthia Rebecca daughter of Mary E.& John Jones born 29th,Nov. 1842, 11 o'clock.

Samuel Swartzwelder born June 10, 1790. Died Aug. 29, 1820.

Cynthia born Sept. 13, 1798 married Feb. 27, 1817.

Bible 1841

Henry M & Eliza Ann Greenleaf married Feb. 13, 1875.

Cynthia Rebecca Grace born March 20, 1876.

SUMNER COUNTY

BIBLE RECORDS

Copied from a Bible owned by "The Seay Family." Bible dated 1851.
Residence North Water St. Gallatin, Tennessee.
Copied by Mrs Alice Guthrie.

Charles N.Talley and Malindy Vance married Dec. 2, 1852.

Charles N Talley born July 13, 1805.

Malindy Vance born Feb. 12, 1816.

Charles J Talley born Jan. 2, 1855.

Tho's E.Summers born July 18, 1859.

Fannie M.Seay born Apr. 8, 1845.

Benjamine Seay born Mar. 26, 1794.

Sarah Wade Seay born Sept. 17, 1800.

Fannie M.Seay died April 11, 1906.

Benjamin Seay born Mar. 9, 1839.

Benjamin Seay married Ella M Shackleford Oct. 4, 1873.

Benjamin Seay and Nannie T Coleman married Dec. 12, 1866.

BIBLE - RECORDS

SUMNER COUNTY
THE THOMASSON FAMILY BIBLE.

Bible belonging to Miss Florence Thomasson. Lives 2½ miles west of Gallatin on Red River Road.
Copied By Alice Baker Gutherie, Summer County, Tennessee
July 23, 1937

Joseph Green Thomasson, Born in Bedford County, Virginia, March 18, 1825.

Elizabeth Louisa Belote, born at Castalian Springs, March 27, 1838.

Joseph Green Thomasson and Elizabeth Louisa Belote, married July 16, 1857. J. R. Graves. M. G.

Joseph Green Thomasson, died March 18, 1897.

Elizabeth Louisa Thomasson, died March 10, 1909

Philip White Hager and Nannie Louisa Thomasson, married November 1880.

SUMNER COUNTY

BIBLE RECORDS

Copied from a Bible dated 1857 owned by Mrs Fred A.Woodward.
Residence West Main St. Gallatin,Tennessee.
Copied by Mrs Alice Guthrie.

John Reid was the father of Mrs F.A.Woodward, he was born April 25,1816, died Aug. 11, 1885.

Maria Frances Thompson his wife, mother of Mrs F.A.Woodward was born Dec. 12, 1832. Died Feb. 14, 1875. Married Oct. 25, 1860.

George Thompson father of Maria Francis Thompson,(her mother(Mary E.B.Keeble both born in the state of Virginia.

George Thompson born May 2, 1805.

Mary Keeble born Mar. 15, 1805.

Harriett R Thompson daughter of George Thompson born Aug. 17, 1827, state of Tennessee, her husband, A.H.Ralston born June 16, 1824 state of Tennessee.

George Thompson married to Mary E.B.Keeble 23 ofNov. 1826 Rutherford County state of Tennessee.

A.H.Ralston married Harriett R.Thompson 6th of June 1856 in Rutherford county state of Tennessee, died 17th, 1868 state of Arkansaw.

SUMNER COUNTY

BIBLE RECORDS

Copied from a bible dated 1856 belonging to J.A.Wemyss given him by Jas. I.Walton Apr. 14,1856.

Residence East Main St. Gallatin,Tennessee.
Copied by Mrs. Walter Witherspoon
November 13,1936.

Alexander Wemyss born in 1794.

Sophia Peck daughter of Abijah & Clarissa Peck born Jan.16,1796., Married in 1822 to Alexander Wemyss. Sophia Peck W. died 1829.
J.Alexander Jan. 20,1823.

Edwin Augustus Aug 18,1824, died Jan. 25,1855.

William died 1836.

SUMNER COUNTY

BIBLE 1852.

Copied from a Bible owned by Mrs Nannie B.Collier.
East Main St. Gallatin,Tennessee.
Copied by Mrs Alice Guthrie.

Nannie Woodward born February 5th, 1858.

Sallie G.Woodward born April 10th, 1859.

F.G.Woodward & C.A.Schluter married December 25th, 1836.

Mrs Annie Woodward born July 12, 1829. Died March 10th 1925.

SUMNER COUNTY

BIBLE RECORDS

Copied from a bible belonging to Mrs. M.D.Working
Residence 2½ miles west of Gallatin, on Long Hollow Pike.
Gallatin,Tennessee.
Copied by Miss Rubye Dillon
November 13,1936.

Henry Working was born Dec. 28,1816

Julia Francis Madden Working was born June 6,1833.

Henry Working departed this life Nov. 8,1888. Aged 72 years,10 months 10 days.

Julia Francis Madden Working departed this life Jan. 25,1912. Aged 79 years 7 months 23 days.

Elizabeth Francis Working was born Dec. 24,1865.

John Thomas Bruce was born Sept. 21,1884.

Martha Lizzabeth Working was born Feb. 26,1880.

Arthur Gerald Working was born Oct. 27,1883.

James Thomas Bruce was married to Amelia Working Jan. 14,1883.

Joseph Working was married to Mary Davis Scott July 31,1878.

William Enoch Working was married to Rosamond Bennett May 1889.

Henry Working was married to his wife Julia Francis on the 6, day of Feb.1859.

Josephus Henry Working was born January 12,1852.

Permelia Malviny was born Aug. 20,1855.

James Turner Working was born April 14,1859.

William Enoch Working was born July 7,1862.

James Turner Working departed this life Aug. 5,1862. Aged 3 years 3 Mo. &22 days

Josephus Henry Working departed this life Oct. 8,1928 Aged 76 years., 9 months & 26 days.

William Enoch Working departed this life May 25th 1929(Nashville,Tenn) Aged 66 years 9 months & 18 days.

SUMNER COUNTY

BIBLE RECORDS

Copied from a bible found in the home of Mrs. M.D.Working.
Residence 2½ miles on Long Hollow Pike west of Gallatin
Owner not known.
Copied by Miss Rubye Dillon
November 13,1936.

W.A.Young, was born Oct. 17,1850.

Willie Potter Young son of W.A.Young & M.J.Young, born August 13,1881, on 3rd St East Nashville,Tenn.

This certifies that the Rite of Holy Matrimony was celebrated between W.A.Young,Horn Lake,Miss and Miss M.J.Porter, Columbia,Tenn on 28th June 1876, was married at Rev. S.Corruthers by Rev.S.Corruthers Columbia Tenn, witness wife & family & neighbors.

SUMNER COUNTY

FAMILY RECORD
CARR FAMILY

The following was copied from a record which is at present in the possession of Alex Carr, who lives about 1 mile west of Hendersonville, and about 13 miles west of Gallatin, Sumner County, Tennessee.

Copied by Miss Rubye Dillon, Gallatin, Tennessee - November 4, 1938.

MARRIAGES

Tolbert Carr and Mary Ann Savely, May 16, 1841
John Utley and May E. Carr, December 26, 1864
James T. Carr and Mollie V. Hall, April 12, 1877
John W. Carr and Elizziebeth P. Brown, October 15, 1874
William H. Savely and Octava T. Carr, October 15, 1874
Dabney W. Carr and Ann Etter Talley, September 31, 1873
William W. Carr and Leamea V. Crunk, October 4, 1874
Thomas A. Cron and Martha A. Carr, August 2, 1877
Alex S. Carr and May E. Talley, December 27, 1883
Charlie C. Carr and Lura Neel, December 26, 1888
Clarence Cron and Mellie Jones, August 12, 1906
Hugh Pryor and Annie Cron, December 23, 1906
Robert Thomas Cron and Bessie Mai Bloodworth, September 15, 1907

BIRTHS

Tolbert Carr, born August 26, 1815
Mary A. Carr, born October 30, 1821
Mary E. Carr, born February 19, 1842
James T. Carr, born December 3, 1844
John W. Carr, born November 25, 1846
Octava T. Carr, born January 25, 1848
Dabney W. Carr, born October 7, 1850
Alexander Carr, born October 18, 1852
Willie W. Carr, born April 21, 1855
Martha Ann Carr, born July 21, 1858
Sallie Smith Carr, born October 21, 1860
Charles Carroll Carr, born July 5, 1863
~~R. T. Carr~~, born August 29, 1883
Ann Etter Carr, born August 7, 1884
R. T. Cron, born August 29, 1883
Clarence Cron, born December 30, 1886
Annie Cron, born May 19, 1889
Branch Cron, born November 26, 1891

DEATHS

Ann Etter Carr, died June 6, 1884 (Note: This date is as written, although her birth is recorded August 7, 1884)
D. W. Carr, died July 6, 1884
Ann Etter Carr, Died August 18, 1885
Tolbert Carr, died September 15, 1887
Mary Ann Carr, died January 12, 1892
Thomas A. Cron, died November 30, 1892
Annie D. Pryor, died July 28, 1907

SUMNER COUNTY

LETTER OF ELWOOD P. CHEEK

This letter was written by Elwood P. Cheek to Mr. and Mrs. L. C. Smith, father and mother of Mrs. Jas. R. Troutt. The letter is at present owned by Mrs. Troutt, who lives at 106 Boyers Street, Gallatin, Sumner County, Tennessee.

Copied by Mrs. Clara M. Harris, Gallatin, Tennessee - June 14, 1939.

Rockspring Jan. 9th 1878

Dear Brother & Sister.

I seat my self to write to you again. I am glad to say we are all well and doing well our relations are all well as far as I know. I seen Mabin day before yesterday he looks about as well as I ever saw him. Martha looks about as well as you ever seen her & Sallies health is very good. Merritte & Florence are well and doing very well. We heard from Calvin about two or three weeks ago they were all enjoying better health except Bedford their address is Janesville Greenwood County Kansas. We are having some very cold weather now crops were tolerable good made 144 bushels of wheat my expences has been heavy this year as the old saying is I can hardly make ends meet. Tell Mrs. Reaves I have got twelve hogs to kill about common size I shall kill next tuesday or wednesday. I have got a good sausage grinder she should have plenty of sausage meat & bisquits & corn bread. John Cate & his family I think is well. I understand he is at work down the County at this time I think they are making out very well I here nothing to the contrery. This letter I think will do for this time write to me often. Tell Charley we raised about 50 or 60 bbls of corn we sold 1,250 lbs of pork at $7.00 per hundred corn is worth 50 cts per bu & flour $6.50 per bbl bacon 8 to 12½ cts ~~lb~~. I have no special news of interest to write. I am still living with Father and expect to remain here as far as I know as he cannot get along well with out some one to help him. Money is very scarce here and almost every thing low. I recon I must close. Write soon remember us in your feeble petitions.

I remain as ever

Yours Truly

Elwood P. Cheek

SUMNER COUNTY

LETTER OF WM. CHEEK

This letter was written by Wm. Cheek to his Daughter, Mrs. L. C. Smith, who was the mother of Mrs. Jas. R. Troutt. The letter is at present in the possession of Mrs. Troutt, who lives at 106 Boyers Street, Gallatin, Sumner County, Tennessee.

Copied by Mrs. Clara M. Harris, Gallatin, Tennessee - June 14, 1939.

December 8, 1872

Well Julia I must answer yours & Luciaus good long Big letter we Recod it in good time. I was very glad to here you was all well. I no dout you are doing well but you must not get too woordlly minded. We are all well but Elwood I think he is mending but very slow. Indeed I have to say to you I have been sorly pressed & for the last twenty years I could keepe my gray head out of the grave. We have been geting a long this year rather poorly but I hope we will do better next year. I have no house keeper of my own now I dont know that I ever shall. I am glad you have not forgoten your old father. Their is nothing in this world that would give me more sorrow than to be treated slightly by my children. Merritt & Elwood & his wife is living with me now but how long I do not know Elwood lost his fine young mare last spring it was a great loss he could have sold her any day for 175. dollars. I have not bought one yet I have not got the money to pay down for a horse. I collected last fall about all that was owing me to pay for this place it cost some 425. dollars. It is all paid now but 20. dollars. Well I will tell you now all our ages I was 69 years old the 22 last September your mother would have been 68 had she lived to the 11th day of last June Calvin was 48 the 4 day of last November Sally was 45 October Martha was 43, 5 November William would have been 41 had he lived to the 27 of this month James Robert was born the 3 of November 1834 Franky was 33 last May Julia was 31 last June the 19 Mabin & Merritt was born 1845 & will be 27 the 31st of January Elwood will be 22 next March the 27th. Well I must write some more but I hardly know what to say this is the driest here I ever saw we have had nothing but light showers since harvest. We made rather light crop of corn. I think we made 144 bushels of wheat. Well Julia I will finish my letter by tellin you I have not tried to get me a wife yet. Mrs. Oldham and some of my neighbors tells me I will have to get me a wife but I dont feel like doing so now but I may possibly have it to do some time if I live. Mabin lives at my old place I have been down their three or four days this week we are diging a well their we have come to hard rock we will have to go to blasting. Elwood is going to move down there when he gets able to work their is plenty of land for both to work on the Hoyd place & the old place. Tell Charley to write to his grandpa.

December 8' 1872
Wm. Cheek

SUMNER COUNTY

RECORD BOOK

The following is a copy of a Record Book belonging to Mrs. Larry Fivash, who lives about 15 miles from Gallatin on the Hendersonville-Shackle Island Road, Sumner County, Tennessee.

Copied by Miss Rubye Dillon, Gallatin, Tennessee - April 12, 1938.

J. R. Coats, born 18th March 1824.

Wm. Hutchison was born in Scotland on the 16th day of March 1790. Died July 6th 1858.

Nancy M. Hartgrove, born January 4th 1797.

Mary Roy Hutchison, born May 4th, 1820.

James Hutchison, born April 5th 1822. Died August 11th 1824.

MARRIAGES

William Hutchison was married to Nancy Mitchel Hartgrove on the 28th July A.D. 1819.

William Hutchison was married to Lucinda Towns Coats on the 20th of October 1836 and divorced on the 15th of October 1851.

SUMNER COUNTY

FAMILY RECORD
McFERRIN FAMILY

The following was copied from a record belonging to Mrs. John A. Soper.

Copied by Mrs. Clara M. Harris, Gallatin, Tennessee, June 30, 1939.

MARRIAGES

John B. McFerrin and Almyra A. Probart were married in Davidson County September 18, 1833 by Rev. A. L. P. Green.
John B. McFerrin and Cynthia Tennessee, daughter of John & Elizabeth B. McGavock, were Married by Rev. W. C. Johnson, November 12th 1855.
John Allen Soper and Mary Almyra Anderson were married December 10th 1902, at Beechland by Rev. John A. McFerrin.
James Anderson & Sarah J. McFerrin were married at Woodlawn, November 15th 1860 by Rev. A. P. McFerrin.
James W. McFerrin and Dora Cooke were married at the residence of her father Watson M. Cooke near Nashville, December 1st, 1868 by Rev. J. P. McFerrin.
John A. McFerrin and Martha D. Abston were married at the residence of her mother Mrs. M. A. Abston, in Sumner County June 28th 1871 by Rev. W. G. Dorris.

BIRTHS

John Berry McFerrin, son of Rev. James McFerrin and Jane C. was born in Rutherford County, Tennessee, June 15, 1807.
Almyra Avery Probart, daughter of William Y. and Sarah Probart, was born in Nashville, Ten., June 20th 1813.
Sarah Jane, daughter of Jno. B. & Almyra A. McFerrin, was born in Nashville, Ten., March 6th 1842, and was baptized by Rev. A.L.P. Green.
James William, son of Jno. B. & A. A. McFerrin, was born in Nashville, Ten., July 14, 1846, and was baptized by Rev. A.L.P. Green, D.D.
John Anderson, son of J. B. & A. A. McFerrin, was born in Nashville, March 26th, 1848, and was baptized by Rev. A.L.P. Green, D.D.
Elizabeth Johnson, daughter of J. B. & A. A. McFerrin, was born at Woodlawn, Davidson County, December 14, 1850 and was baptized by Rev. A. L.P. Green, Doctor of Divinity.
Almyra Probart, daughter of J. B. & A. A. McFerrin, was born at Woodlawn, Davidson County, Ten., May 8th 1854 and was baptized by Bishop J. Soule.
Cynthia Tennessee, daughter of John & Elizabeth B. McGavock, was born at Fountaine Blean near Nashville, Tenn., July 26th 1827.
Kittie Lou, daughter of J. B. & C. T. McFerrin, was born at Woodlawn December 24, 1856 at 3 o'clock P.M. she was baptized by Bishop J.O. Andrew.
Mary McGinly McGavock, daughter of J. B. & C. T. McFerrin, was born at Woodlawn, March 1, 1859 she was baptized by her father a short time before her death.

Elizabeth McGavock, daughter of J. B. & C. T. McFerrin, was born at Woodlawn July 23rd 1861 and was baptized by Rev. James R. McClure.

Children of James and Sarah Jane Anderson
John McFerrin Anderson born, June 20th 1862. Baptized by his grandfather John B. McFerrin May 19, 1863.
William Wade Anderson, born May 19th 1864 baptized by his grandfather June 15, 1865.
James Douglass Anderson, born October 6th 1867, baptized by his grandfather March 6, 1870.
Walter Leak Anderson, born December 4th 1869, baptized by his grandfather March 6th, 1870.
Ewell Avery Anderson, born December 31, 1871, baptized by his grandfather July 11th 1872.
Mary Almyra Anderson, born November 28, 1873, baptized by her grandfather June 24, 1872.
Virginia Lou Anderson, born November 1st 1875, baptized by her grandfather October 14, 1877.
Dora Anderson, born March 22, 1878, baptized by her grandfather July 26, 1878.
Frank Weakley Anderson, born March 30, 1883, baptized by his grandfather June 20, 1883.
Jane Parrish Anderson, born October 4, 1886, baptized by her grandfather in East Nashville.
Mc, Wade, Douglass, and Walter were born in Davidson County, the rest at "Beechland" Home in Sumner County, Tennessee.

William Anderson Soper, son of John and Mary Anderson Soper, born June 14, 1905.
Elizabeth Soper, daughter of John and Mary Anderson Soper, born August 6, 1906
John Allen Soper, son of John and Mary Anderson Soper, born April 24, 1910.

DEATHS

Died in peace at Woodlawn May 12th 1854 near 6 o'clock P.M. Almyra A. McFerrin wife of J. B. McFerrin. She had been a Methodist twenty-two years. A good wife, a fond mother and a woman of sterlin virtue.
Elizabeth Johnson, daughter of J. B. McFerrin and A. A. McFerrin, died at Woodlawn July 20, 1854. We called her Bettie, she was a beautiful, sweet child.
Mary McGinty McGavock, daughter of J. B. and C. T. McFerrin, died at A. F. McFerrin's near Woodbury, Ten. August 18, 1859. Her mother was on a visit when her child sickened and died. Her body was brought home and interred.
Jas. W. McFerrin, son of Rev. J. B. & A. A. McFerrin, died November 16th 1880, 1 o'clock P.M. Killed in a R.R. wreck at Birmingham, Ala.
Ewell Anderson, son of Jas. and Sarah McFerrin Anderson, Nov. 26, 1899.
James Anderson, died March 16, 1902.
Dora Anderson, died October 14, 1902.

Died in Christian triumph at his residence in northeast Nashville, May 10th 1887 at 1: A.M. John Berry McFerrin in his 79th year.
William Anderson Soper, died July 1st 1906.
Sarah McFerrin Anderson, died September 6th 1906.
Janie Parrish Anderson, died May 1930, daughter of James and Sarah McFerrin Anderson.
John McFerrin Anderson, son of James and Sarah McFerrin Anderson, died December 31, 1933.

Children and Grandchildren of Rev. Jas. & Mrs. Jane C. McFerrin

1st Child John Berry - his children - 1st nameless, died at the age of 10 days. 2nd Sarah Jane, 3rd James William, 4th John Anderson, 5th Elizabeth Johnson, dead, 6th Almyra Probart, 7th Kittie Lou, 8th Mary McGavock, dead, 9th Bettie McGavock.

2nd Child William Meek, his children - 1st Minerva Jane, dead, 2nd John Henderson, 3rd Mary Lavinia, dead, 4th William Anderson, dead, 5th Melville Sommerfield, 6th Mattie Lou, dead, 7th Sallie Walker, 8th Iverson, dead, 9th Malinda Jessie, dead, 10th James Benj. dead.

3rd Child Thomas Berry died at 8 months

4th Child Eliza Campbell, married first to Mr. N. Smith, and secondly to Rev. Saml. Gilliland, Dead. Her children 1st Martha Jane, dead, 2nd Mary Frances, dead, 3rd Almyra Probart, 4th Ann Eliza, dead, 5th Sallie Emily, 6th Jas. McFerrin, 7th John Williams, 8th Alice Amanda, 9th Ella Louisa, 10th Samuel, dead.

5th Child James Henderson, his children, 1st Lavinia Jane, 2nd Mary Ann, 3rd Florence Augusta.

6th Anderson Purdy, his children, 1st John Porter, 2nd Mary Elizabeth, 3rd Thomas Sumner, 4th Jane, 5th Anderson Purdy, 6th Nameless dead, 7th William James, 8th Minnie, 9th Lillie, 10th Porter, 11th Marvin.

7th Child Nancy Jane, married Mr. John Applewhite. Her children, 1st Louisa Elizabeth, 2nd James Isaac, 3rd Minerva Jane, 4th John Keen, 5th Emma Rebecca, 6th Sallie Eliza, 7th Fletcher McFerrin, 8th Willie Lelia, dead, 9th Irvine Henderson, dead, 10th Edgar Lee.
Grand Children 53.
Great Grand Children up to March 1873, 44. 1 Great, Great, Grand Child.

SUMNER COUNTY

FAMILY RECORD
SHANE FAMILY

The following was copied from a record belonging to S. M. Sweeney, who lives 3 miles from Hendersonville, Tennessee, on Waltons Ferry Road, and about 14 miles west of Gallatin, Sumner County, Tennessee.

Copied by Miss Rubye Dillon, Gallatin, Tennessee - August 22, 1938.

BIRTHS

John Shane was born May 22, 1789 and was married to Nancy Drennon August 15, 1819 on Sunday.
Nancy Drennon was born May the 5, 1795.
Polly Drennon Shane was born February the 17th 1813.
Amanda M. Shane was born February the 18th on Sunday morning 1821.
Almoreen Shane was born in the year 1822 July the 30th on Tuesday.
Ebinaide Shane was born April the 9th 1825 on Saturday about sundown.
Araminty Shane was born July the 15th 1826 on Friday night.
John Shane, Jun. was born February the 15th 1828 on Friday morning.
Ann Shane was born August the 10th 1830 on Munda knight.
Osmon Shane was born April the 15th 1831, Saturday morning.
William Shane was born December the 15th day on Friday morning 1832.
Marianna Shane was born December the 20th 1834 on Saturday night.
Ann the youngest of the daughters was born the 4th June 1858.

DEATHS

Ebinaide departed this life February the 22d 1841, lived 16 years 10 months and 15 days.
Marrianna departed this life the 30th September 1846. She was eleven years 8 months and 20 days olde when she died.
Osmon Shane departed this life November the 6th 1847.
Ann Jenkins departed this life July 16th 1858 on Friday at 3 oclock.
Rolly Michel departed this life in May 1859
Araminty departed this life December 11, 1859.
John Shane was killed near Atlanty Georgy on the 22nd July 1864.
John Shane, Sr. died June 26, 1876.
Nancy Shane died November 11, 1878.

FAMILY RECORD
SWEENEY FAMILY

The following was copied from a record belonging to S. M. Sweeney, who lives 3 miles from Hendersonville, Tennessee, on Waltons Ferry Road, and about 14 miles west of Gallatin, Sumner County, Tennessee.

Copied by Miss Rubye Dillon, Gallatin, Tennessee - August 22, 1938.

BIRTHS

Joseph Sweeney was born 16th of June 1849.
Annie Jenkins was born the 4th of June 1858.
Sylvester Mortimer Sweeney was born the 9th of October 1874.
Florence Pearl Sweeney was born the 23rd of February 1880.
Howell Fields Sweeney was born November the 30th 1889.
Arthur Earls was born July the 12, 1878.
Maude Jenkins was born September 17, 1876.

MARRIAGES

Joseph Sweeney and Annie Jenkins were married 6th of April 1873.
Arthur Earls and Florence Pearl Sweeney were maried the 5th of February 1899.
Sylvester Mortimer Sweeney and Maude Jenkins were married September 28, 1898 at the home of Lell Jenkins in Wilson County.

SUMNER COUNTY

FAMILY RECORD
TALLEY FAMILY

The following was copied from a record which is at present in the possession of Mrs. Alex Carr, who lives about 1 mile west of Hendersonville, Tennessee, and 12 miles west of Gallatin, Sumner County, Tennessee.

Copied by Miss Rubye Dillon, Gallatin, Tennessee - May 6, 1938.

BIRTHS & MARRIAGES

William Anderson Talley, born October 31, 1798, was married to Polly Ann Dowdy 1820.

James T. Talley was born October 7, 1822. Married December 1847 to Elizabeth K. Sauley. Saxeh

Naney E. Talley, born April 4, 1824.

Elizabeth A. Talley, born December 19, 1825. Married December 17, 1845 to Allen Pryor.

Burlington B. Talley, born October 8, 1827.

Lucy H. Talley, born January 11, 1829. Married to Robert Wright 1870.

Sally F. Talley, born November 2, 1830. Married James Byram.

Catherine H. Talley, born April 2, 1832.

John D. Talley, born May 21, 1834.

Mary J. Talley, born September 17, 1836.

Permelia Ann Talley, born April 22, 1838. Married to Thomas Pryor 1871.

1st wife of Gen. S.R. Anderson

SUMNER COUNTY

ANDERSON
TOMBSTONE INSCRIPTIONS

Cemetery, 3 miles on Long Hollow Pike from Gallatin, Tennessee
Residence of Mrs Ewing Hite Gallatin, Tenn.
Copied by Mrs Alice Guthrie.

Consecrated by a friend to the memory of Susan M. Anderson, born Feb.22,1799 died July 23, 1841.

Miller
Miller

"Let me die the death of the righteous
And let my last end be like theirs."

H.E.Jones born April 5, 1788 died April 30, 1819.
"I would not live always
No welcome the tomb
Since Jesus hath laid there I dread not its gloom
Then sweet be my rest
Till he bid me arise
To hail him in triumph
Decending the skies."

To the memory of Elizabeth Carter wife of Washington Carter, daughter of John & Susanah Miller born Aug. 31st 1801. Married Sept. 18, 1825. Departed this life Feb. 10, 1842.

"Happy soul thy days are ended
All thy mourning days below
Go by angles guards attended
To the sight of Jesus go
This tree a sacred monument rear
Whose weeping boughs
Wave over thy resting place
And shall in future years
Tell me that thou art here
Resting in silence
In thy dark abode
When friends unite
To walk deaths Common road
Elizabeth farewell, farewell
Tis Jesus calls thee home
My bleeding heart submits
His will be done Elizabeth farewell,
farewell.

TOMBSTONE - INSCRIPTIONS

BAKER-PARSON CEMETERY
SUMNER COUNTY

Located 4 miles East of Gallatin, Tennessee, in private graveyard, on Cairo Road. Graveyard known as the "Baker-Parson Cemetery".
There are two markers with names only: Pruett and Cox.
All stones are field stones.
There are 50 field stones.
Copied by Mrs. Alice Guthrie, Gallatin, Tennessee.
March 19, 1937.

TOMBSTONE - INSCRIPTIONS

BARNES
SUMNER COUNTY

Tomb located in the front lot of place owned by
Mr. Jim Bohanan, 3½ miles West of Gallatin, Tenn.,on
Long Hollow Pike.
Copied by Mrs. Alice Guthrie, Gallatin, Tennessee.
April 22, 1937.

Nathan Barnes,
Departed this Life,
Jan. 29, 1827.
Age 57 years.

SUMNER COUNTY

BARRY
TOMBSTONE INSCRIPTIONS

Tombs located in field of hôme of Harry Stiltz, on Nashville Pike.
Gallatin, Tennessee.
Copied by Mrs Alice Guthrie.

Franklin Barry, born _____of Dec. Died at day break the 19th day of __1856.

Margaret Jane Barry born Feby 15, 1834. Died Aug. 20, 1834.
"Suffer little children to come unto me for of such is the Kingdom of Heaven."

Sacred to the memory of Jane Barry born 19th Oct.1780, married 25th Dec. 1803 age 60 years & 5 months.
" Blessed are the dead which die in the Lord
From hence fourth yea with the Spirit
That they may rest from their labor
And their works do follow them."

In memory of Dr. Redmond Barry, a native of Ireland, he was born Dec. 22, 1766, and died Feb. 10th, 1821. Age 55 years 1 month & 25 days.

William A Barry born March 25th 1805. Died May 13th, 1805.

John B Barry born May 29, 1806. Died July 6, 1806. Infants.

Thomas Barry Jr, son of Tho's & Sarah H Barry born Feb. 15th 1840. Died Oct. 11th, 1854.

Sarah H Barry wife of Thomas Barry born Oct. 17, 1810. Died May 7, 1876.

SUMNER COUNTY

BATE
TOMBSTONE INSCRIPTIONS

Cemetery, 8 miles from the town of Gallatin, Tennessee.
In yard of Old Bate home, owned by Brimmage Bate Castalian Springs
Copied by Mrs Alice Guthrie.

In memory of James H.Bate was born 25th Nov. 1804. Died 14th April 1842. 32 years, 4 months, 19 days.

SUMNER COUNTY

BEECH CHURCH
TOMBSTONE INSCRIPTIONS

Beech Church, located on LongHollow Pike 10 miles west of Gallatin.
Gallatin,Tennessee.
Copied by Mrs.Alice Guthrie.

Hannah,W.T.Jouett died July 24,1820. Age 41 years.

Daniel Montgomery, born March 25, 1789,Died July 5, 1855.

William Montgomery, born Sept. 21, 1762,died Sept. 15, 1838. Age 76 years.

Jane Montgomery consort of William Montgomery, Age 73 years, born March 8, 1837.

Sarah Montgomery consort of Daniel Montgomery, died July 7, 1850. Age 55 years.

Margaret M. Smith, born Aug. 4, 1822,died July 27, 1848.

Jane McMillin, died 1806. Age 75 years.

Cathrine, wife of J.R.Hutchinson,born March 24, 1828, died Oct.1, 1889.

J.R.Hutchinson, born March 12, 1826, died Feb. 10, 1894.

Mr. James Reid, died Aug. 14, 1838. Age 75 years.

Wm. J.Montgomery, born May 20,1824,died May 3, 1875.

John Montgomery, born April 17,1826;died Han.22, 1889.

Peter Ketring, born April 26,1775.Died Mar.13,1866.

Jane Ketring consort of Peter Ketring bonn Sept. 23, 1796, died Sept. 21, 1849.

Francis Ketring, died July 1819. Age 71 years.

Wm.Lowry, born 1800,died July 29, 1815.

Barnet Hauk, died 1817. Age 87 years.

Francis Kirkpatrick, born Nov.1, 1774, died Sept. 15,1850.

Alexander Kirkpatrick, born March 1772, died Dec.1807.

John Kirkpatrick, born April 1770, died Oct.10,1806.

John McMurtrey Esq. died March 16,1841, Age 89 years.

Margaret McMurtrey, born Aug.1, 1763, died Apr. 4, 1846.

W.J.Frazer, born Aug. 13, 1821, died July 21, 1888.

John Boyd, died Jan.3, 1846, aged 20 years.

Cyrus Boyd, born Jan.28, 1806, died Feb. 17, 1879.

William King, born Jan. 17, 1777, died Sept. 9, 1842.

Daniel King, born Dec. 16, 1820, died June 19, 1846.

A.Hogan, born Jan.26, 1802, Died July 24, 1893.

Rebecca Hogan, born Dec. 6, 1806, died July 19, 1847.

James H.Hogan, "A volenteer in the Mexican War" born Dec. 28,1825
Died Aug. 23, 1848.

John W.Hogan, born Nov. 21,1830, died Sept. 24, 1858.

John Kizer, died Jan. 12, 1860, age 65 years.

John W.Garrett, born Feb.2, 1312, died Mar. 10,1891.

James Elizer, born Apr. 8,1798, died Feb. 1875.

Joseph Kirkpatrick, born Ded. 21, 1827, died Dec.11, 1845.

Samuel Kirkpatrick, born Nov. 20, 1798, died Sept. 11, 1853.

James Kirkpatrick, born July 18, 1768, died Nov. 24, 1852.

Rev. Hugh Kirkpatrick, born May 8, 1771, died Dec. 3, 1863.

Stewart Kirkpatrick, born Apr. 15, 1802, died Mar. 20, 1844.

Samuel Kirkpatrick, born Jan.6, 1800, died June 27, 1875.

Robert Taylor, born Mar. 11, 1777, died Mar. 30, 1859.

at least 300 more graves with markers.

SUMNER COUNTY

BETHPAGE
TOMBSTONE INSCRIPTIONS

Bethpage Cemetery, located 10 miles east of Gallatin on the Scottsville Pike Gallatin, Tennessee.
Copied by Miss Ruby Dillon.
November 16,1936.

Sacred to the memory of John Doak Hanna, born May 29 A.D.1801. Died April 5,A.D.1833.

Sacred to the memory of Susan Hanna Senr. born May 17,1775, died July 22,1840.
" In hope of a Blest immortality."

Sacred to the memory of James Hanna, born June 15,A.D.1765, died March 29,A.D.1833.

Sacred to the memory of Sarah Brison, born Jan. 19, A.D.1790, died Oct. 3,A.D.1821.

Sacred to the memory of James Bryson, born Nov.28,A.D.1745, died Sept., 3,A.D.1835.

To the memory of W.P.Woodson, born Feb. 6,1832, died April 23,1855.

To the memory of John M.Woodson, born Dec. 25,1835, died May 7,1854.

Elizabeth, wife of Dr. T.M.Woodson born Apr. 18,1832, died Aug. 19,1854.
Also her infant Ivone Miller. Aged 7 months.

Lucinda, wife of Rev. L.M.Woodson born Dec. 7,1803,died May 8,1872.
" She was a kind and affectionate Mother, her smiles cast their rays of Cheerfulness through our household, she has gone to her reward to live with God, forever."

Bettie M Brown, daughter of Rev. L.M. and L.Woodson born Aug.10,1839, died April 20, 1866.

James A.Staley, born Aug. 14,1877, died Dec. 9,1887.

Mollie E.Turner, born Oct. 6,1832, died Sept. 5,1866.

Mary Martin, born Aug. 10,1807, died April 11,1872.

Sacred to the memory of Abraham Martin, born April 13,1795,died Jan.29,1861.
Aged 65 years nine months and 16 days.

Martha A Carr, born May 11,1828, died June 25,1851.

In memory of James G.,son of J.S.& Martha Carr born July 21,1824,died Aug. 5,1855.

SUMNER COUNTY

TOMBSTONE INSCRIPTIONS

John S.Carr, born Nov. 30,1800, died May 21,1872.
" Oh Man upon thy doom
And wisdom's lesson learn,
Tis but a sleep unto the tomb,
Where You'll to dust return."

Martha, wife of John S.Carr born Mar. 19,1799, died Aug. 5,1881.
" A faithful wife A mother dear
In sweet repose is sleeping here
Her painful loss we deeply feel
But God can all our sorrows heal".

Willie May, daughter of W.T. & Susan A.Rickman born Feb. 27,1861, died Oct. 6,1863.

Elvina S.Vance, born May the 8,1824, died July the 2,1854.
" Her infant Babe Sarah."

William M.Malone, born Jan 31,1817, died Dec. 5, 1830.
Son of James & Margaret Malone.

Field Stones - 40

SUMNER COUNTY

TOMBSTONE INSCRIPTIONS

Bethpage Cemetery, located 10 miles east of Gallatin on Scottsville Pike.
Gallatin, Tennessee.
Copied by Mrs. Walter Witherspoon
November 16,1936.

Alexander Dillihay, born November 8,1818, died June 19,1878.

Hugh D.Long born Jan.23,1820, died June 20,1879.

Rufus K.Hodges, born May 23,1856, died Sept. 7,1888.

Taylor Louis, born Jan.15,1826, died May 21,1896.

William Gillespie, born Feb. 3,1803, died July 1,1897. Age 94 years-4Mo.& 28 days.

James N.Malone, born Jan.5,1806, died Dec. 31,1884.

Sue G.Staley,born June 28,1844, died Jan. 28,1880.

William Whiteside, born Feb. 17,1777, died Oct. 3,1844.

Jane P.Gillespie, born Mar. 17,1805,died July 12,1872.

Alfred Morgan Black, born May 6,1849, died Feb. 24,1892.

Joseph Chipman, born Mar. 16,1818,died Dec. 9,1862.

James H.Key, born Aug. 8,1840, died Feb. 9,1862.
"A volunteer in defence of his Country."

Robert W.Loide, born Jan.__ 1829, died Oct. 9,1889.

Armstead Moore, born June 1,1814,died November 7,1884.

Daniel McCaughy, born Mar. 8,1793, died Feb. 22,1839.

Nathaniel P.Parker, born March 17,1775, died Jan. 15,1858.

Lucretia Parker, born ___ Died Feb. 25,1860. Age 88 years.

Robert W.Durham, born Oct. 15,1832, died Mar. 28,1879.

Dr. J.B.Hanna ____ ____died Feb. 24,1912. Age 65 years.

Field Stones - 75.

SUMNER COUNTY

TOMBSTONE INSCRIPTIONS

Tombs located in Cemetery at Bethpage,Tenn. 10 miles east of Gallatin on the Scottsville Pike.
Gallatin,Tennessee.
Copied by Mrs. Alice Guthrie. Date: November 16, 1936.

Rebecca H. wife of Rev. J.G.Ray born July 13,1817, married Feb. 16,1836 died Nov. 30,1906.
"Home at Last."

Rev. J.G.Ray, born July 9,1818, died Oct. 5,1896.
" I have fought a good fight
I have finished my course
I have kept the faith."

Patsy Carr, born March 24,1812, died Dec. 28,1821.
" Blessed are the dead who die in the Lord."

In memory of Jno Carr, born in South Carolina Sept.5,1773, He was a citizen of Sumner County 73 years.
A Patriot he served in the war of 1812
Truly an honest man. Sixty years a consistent Methodist. Died Dec. 31, 1858 age 85 years.

Sarah Carr wife of Jno Carr, born June 29,1774 died Aug. 23, 1841.
" Rest Mother rest in quiet sleep
While friends in sorrow o'er thee weep."

William C.Carr, born Jan. 17 1798, Died June 5,1835.
" He lived beloved and died lamented."

Rev. Jno.Parker, born Aug. 17,1792, died Feb. 4,1866.
A minister of the Gospel 49 years. His wife Polly born Mar.15,1796 died Mar. 10,1866, They were married Feb. 21,1815. Two Christians Pleasant in their lives in death not divided.

Jno. W.Ray, born May 16,1813, died July 18,1868.

W.S.Whitesides, born May 25,1820, died Feb. 18,1881.

William B.Key, born Dec. 24,1814, Died Oct. 29, 1889.

Jno Senter, born March 4,1796, died Jan. 6,1882.

Rhoda, wife of Jno.Senter born 1798, died Aug. 16,1889.

Amanda White, wife of W.B.Key, born Feb.24,1821, died Jan. 10,1892.

William Whitesides, born Feb. 17, 1777, died Oct. 3,1844.

Blanch Whitesides, born Jan. 16,1787, died Sept. 29,1849.

SUMNER COUNTY

TOMBSTONE INSCRIPTIONS

Thomas Whitesides, born May 29,1815, died Feb. 21,____A.D.

Rev. Jno.Parker, born Aug. 17,1792 died Feb. 4,1866. A Minister of the Gospel 49 years.
His wife Polly born Mar.15, 1796, died Mar.10,1866.
"They were married Feb 21,1815. Two Christians
"Pleasant in their lives in death not devided."

John W.Ray, born May 16,1813 died July 18,1868.

W.S.Whitesides, born May 25,1820 died Feb.18,1881.

William B.Key, born Dec.24,1814, died Oct. 29,1889.

Nathaniel Parker Sr., born Mar. 17,1775, died Jan. 15,1856.

In memory of Lucretia wife of Nathaniel Parker, died Feb 25,1860. Aged about 83 years.

Robt. W. Durham, born Oct. 15,1832, died Mar. 28,1879.

In memory of Lee Hanna, born Aug. 26,1810, died May 27, 1871.
" He sleeps in Jesus."

J.B.Hanner Sr., born Feb. 13,1797, died Aug. 30,1875.

Rev. Luke P.Allen, born in State of Virginia Aug. 1,1735 died in Allen County Kentucky Dec. 18,1845.

Mrs. Aramita D, wife of Rev. L.P.Allen born in Butler County Kentucky Feb. 24, 1814, died Apr. 27,1904.

100 Field stones.

SUMNER COUNTY

BLACKEMORE
TOMBSTONE INSCRIPTIONS.

Tombs located in field of Paul Stewart on Coles Ferry Pike 6 miles south of Gallatin, Tennessee.
Copied by Mrs. Alice Guthrie. November 16, 1936.

J.T.Blackemore, born Apr. 8,1822, died June 2,1914.

Mary E.Darnell, wife of J.T.Blakemore born Dec. 26,1819, died Apr. 22, 1888.

SUMNER COUNTY

BLEDSOE ACADEMY
TOMBSTONE INSCRIPTIONS

Cemetery, Bledsoe Academy 7½ miles from Gallatin,Tenn.
Castalian Springs, Tennessee.
Copied by Mrs Alice Guthrie.

Wm Baskerville born April 10, 1812. Died Marl 30, 1885.

Mrs Mary Baskerville born Nov. 11, 1807, died March 14, 1866 aged 58 years 4 mo & 4 days.

Sacred to the memory of Martha Goode daughter of Martha Baskerville, born on the 10th of Sept 1840 departed this life July 26, 1855.

Charles D.Beeler born Sept 1732, died March 1749.

In memory of Mrs Lucy Cornwell consort of Enoch L Cornwell born Sept. 27, 1812. departed this life June 9, 1855.

In memory of Sarah C Patton consort of Thos Patton was born June 12th, 1822 died June 28, 1850.

SUMNER COUNTY

BLOODWORTH-PARKER
TOMBSTONE INSCRIPTIONS

Cemetery, located 3½ miles west of Gallatin on Long Hollow Pike.
Residence of W.H.Keisling, Gallatin,Tennessee.
Copied by Mrs Alice Guthrie.

Mary B.Bloodworth, born Dec.3, 1861. Died Sept. 20, 1887.

Mrs Susan Elizabeth Parker, consort of S.C.Parker departed this life Septl, 1831. Age 20 years, 6 months & 10 days."Depart My friends and dry your tears, I must lie here Till Christ appears."

Here sleeps the body of Mrs Cherry Ellis, consort of The Rev.Joseph Ellis, who died June 16, 1852 in the morning. Age __ yr's 2 mo. & 25 days.
"Why do we mourn for departing friends
Or shake at deaths alarm
Tis but the voice of Jesus
That calls them to Heaven."

Sacred to the memory of Hardy M.Parker died July 19, 1852.

SUMNER COUNTY

BRADLEY
TOMBSTONE INSCRIPTIONS

Cemetery, located on Dobbins pike 15 miles from Gallatin,
Gallatin, Tennessee.
Copied by Mrs Alice Guthrie.

Richard Bradley born Oct. 27, 1824. Died Feb. 19, 1897.

Purdence Jane Bradley born Jan. 8, 1844. Died Mar. 31, 1904.
" Gone but not forgottne."

Madison A.Buck born Oct. 6, 1839. Died Sept. 27, 1907.

S.T.Reddick born Aug. 16, 1834.

Esom Cron born Dec. 19, 1811. Died Apr. 5, 1818.
"Blessed are the pure in heart for they shall see God."

Penelope Jane, wife of F.G.Durham born Oct. 19, 1844. Died July 5, 1909.

Susan R.Bradley born Oct. 15, 1824. Died May 9, 1891.

John A Reddick born Dec. 1, 1811. Died Nov. 10, 1874.

Milly Hodges, born July 19, 1793. Died Sept. 15, 1879.

B.L.Gregory, born Apr. 22, 1846. Died July 2, 1910.

SUMNER COUNTY

BROWN
TOMBSTONE INSCRIPTIONS

Cemetery, located 4 miles west of Gallatin on Long Hollow Pike.
Residence of Old Barton Brown's Home Gallatin,Tennessee.
Copied by Mrs Alice Guthrie.

Rev. B.B.Brown, born June 26, 1798. Died June 24, 1874.

SUMNER COUNTY

BUSH
TOMBSTONE INSCRIPTIONS

Cemetery, located 5 miles on Long Hollow Pike from Gallatin.
Residence of W.C.Creasey Farm, Gallatin,Tennessee.
Copied by Mrs Alice Guthrie.

W.A.Bush born Aug. 13, 1821. Died June 22, 1907.

Harriett Bush born May 25, 1833. Died June 23, 1908.
" At Rest."

In memory of John Murphy, born A.D.1745. Departed this life July 8,1825, Age 80 years.

SUMNER COUNTY

Tombstone Inscriptions

CAGE

Cemetery, located in lot of place knows as Dr.C.Robbins 8 miles from Gallatih, Tennessee on Cages Bend Road.
Copied by Mrs Alice Guthrie.

Sophia W.Franklin born Nov.25,1809, Died Dec. 22, 1833.

Orvillel Cage, born Aug. 30,1800,died Oct. 5, 1859.
"He was the friend of God & Man."

Louisa Cage, born Mar. 22, 1821, died Oct. 30,1840. Married Oct.18,1838.
" Was a tender and devoted wife, Mother of three children and for six years an acceptable member of the Methodist Church."

Reuben Cage, born July 22, 1772, died June 30, 1853.

SUMNER COUNTY

CALLENDER
TOMBSTONE INSCRIPTIONS

Tombs located in field of farm known as the Old Saunders home, 10 miles west of Gallatin on the Nashville Pike near Hendersonville,Tenn. Gallatin, Tennessee.
Copied by Mrs. Alice Guthrie.

Anna Lizzia, aged 13 years.

Ada Turner, aged 1 year, children of C.W. & Clara Callender died July 27,1855.
" Our little Harper."

101

TOMBSTONE - INSCRIPTIONS

CONGER
SUMNER COUNTY

Graves in field on place owned by Mr. V.J.Mitchell, 8½ miles East of Gallatin, Tennessee, on Station Camp Creek Road.
Copied by Mrs. Alice Guthrie, Gallatin, Tenn.
April 1, 1937.

S. Maggie, Wife of
James Conger,
Born March 17, 1855.
Died Sept. 21, 1905.

Charlotte Brigance,Wife of
J. F. Crabb,
Born April 9, 1852.
Died Sept. 28, 1903.

J. F. Crabb,
Born June 22, 1836.
Died Sept. 1, 1907.

Wiley B. Brigham,
Born Oct. 2, 1814.
Died March 26, 1895.

Wiley E. Corbitt,
Died Jan. 1, 1901.
Age 25 years.

Mrs. Francis Corbitt,
Born Jan. 6, 1836.
Died Mar. 1, 1899.

(Field Stones 14)

SUMNER COUNTY

COTTON
TOMBSTONE INSCRIPTIONS

Cemetery, located 7 miles west of Gallatin, Tennessee.
Residence of George Parham, Cotton, Tennessee.
Copied by Mrs Alice Guthrie.

In memory of Benj F. Sutton born 1807. Died Sept. 21, 1850.

Lovel Sutton, born Feby 11, 1804. Died June 15, 1852.

Polly Payne, born May 27, 1830. Died May 27, 1850.

Marshall N. Payne, born Apr. 17, 1848. Died Aug. 1848.

Moore Cotton, Born Dec. 27, 1771, died Dec. 13, 1836.

William Cotton, born July 28, 1832. Died Mar. 13, 1833.

Alexander Cotton, Born Oct. 23, 1814. Died Sept. 12, 1834.

Thomas C. Hobday, born May 29, 1835. Died Oct. 15, 1836.

Andrew M. Hobday, born Mar. 25, 1837. Died June 12, 1837.

Hugh Cotton, Born Feb. 19, 1807. Died Aug. 21, 1849.

Richard D Hobdy (a inserted by hand: Hobday), born Apr. 22, 1794. Died July 2, 1851.

A. Parham, born Dec. 14, 1825. died Mar. 1, 1902.

Lovey Rogers, wife of Alexander Parham born Oct. 18, 1837. Died Jan. 30, 1914.

SUMNER COUNTY

CRUMPLY
TOMBSTONE INSCRIPTIONS

Tombs located in field of Johnson Dyer, Lock 4 Road 4 miles south of Gallatin, Tennessee.
Copied by Mrs. Alice Guthrie. November 16, 1936.

William Crumply, born Nov. 22, 1820 died Feb. 7,1824.

44 Field Stones.

Some Indian Graves.

Place formerly owned by Isaac Franklin.

SUMNER COUNTY

CRYER
TOMBSTONE INSCRIPTIONS

Cemetery, on Long Hollow Pike at home of Mrs Roy Vantrease
Gallatin,Tennessee.
Copied by Mrs Alice Guthrie.

Mrs Nancy C Roscoe died Mar. 15, 1830 in the 28th year of her age.
" She was an abediant wife, an affectionate & kind mother
A faithful & tryumphant Christian
Give Joy or grief
Give ease or_____
Take life or friends away
But let me find them all again
In that eternal day."

To the memory of the Lamented and much beloved Martha Cryer, died Oct. 11th, 1832.

Sacred to the memory of James Cryer."A Revolutionary soldier and an honest man." died the 12th, Mar. 1816.
In hopes of a blessful imortality through Jesus Christ.

Henry Lucas Collier, son of V.L.& S.E.Collier born Feb. 3, 1849, died Feb. 16, 1849.
" Suffer little children to come unto me and forbid them not
For of such is the kingdom of Heaven."

Susan Elizabeth wife of Vines L.Collier born Jan. 25, 1830, died Apr. 29th, 1861.
" For I know that my redeemer liveth
And that he shall stand at the day upon the earth
And though after the skin worms destroy this body and my flesh,
I shall see God."

SUMNER COUNTY

DARNELL- HAMILTON
TOMBSTONE INSCRIPTIONS

Tombs located in field of James Green on Coles Ferry Pike, 3 miles east of Gallatin, Tennessee.
Copied by Mrs. Alice Guthrie. November 16, 1936.

Emma Gregory, born Mar.9,1851, died June 11, 1884.

James Hamilton, died Mar. 20,1875. Age 89 years.

Jane Taylor Hamilton, 2nd wife of James Hamilton died Aug. 7,1873. Age 71 years.

Leonora Hamilton, wife of F,D. Escue born July 9,1842, died May 26,1878.

Francis Darnell, born Oct. 29,1813, died Jan. 8,1888.

A.H. Halbert, born Oct. 31,1811, died Sept. 8,1889.

J.S.Darnell, born Dec. 11,1786, died Dec. 4,1852.

TOMBSTONE - INSCRIPTIONS

DOUGLASS GRAVEYARD
SUMNER COUNTY

Located in a field on place owned by Mrs.W.S.Grimm, 9 miles West of Gallatin, Tenn.,on Station Camp Creek Road. Copied by Mrs. Alice Guthrie, Gallatin, Tennessee. April 13, 1937.

To the Memory of
Malissa Douglass,Daughter of
Reubin & Elizabeth Douglass,
Born May 21, 1802.
Died June 22, 1862.

Eliza L. Wife of
W. J. Douglass,
Born May 23, 1802.
Died Sept. 13, 1835.

Willie J. Douglass,
Born Sept. 21, 1792.
Died Mar. 18, 1866.

To the Memory of
W. M. Franklin,
Born Sept. 15, 1784.
Died Oct. 31, 1876.
Age 82 yrs.

Eveline Franklin,Wife of
W. M. Franklin,
Born Jan. 23, 1799.
Died Apr. 14, 1855.

To the Memory of
Elizabeth Douglass,Wife of
Reubin Douglass,Daughter of
William & Sara Edwards,
Born June 25, 1774.
Departed this Life,
Jan. 9, 1859.

To the Memory of
Reubin Douglass,
Born Apr. 6, 1767.
Died Aug. 26, 1832.

William Richard Douglass,
Born June 24, 1808.
Died Apr. 5, 1829.

Sacred to the Memory of
The Rev.William S.F.Clark,
Who came Hither,
Jan. 6, 1806.
And went Home,
Aug. 16, 1847.

Emma Clark,
Born Aug. 21, 1806.
Died Dec. 10, 1881.

Reubin Clark,
Born Aug. 28, 1834.
Died Dec. 29, 1864.

Ellen Clark Brown,
Born Dec. 16, 1845.
Died Jan. 2, 1928.

Alfred D. Brown,
Died Feb. 7, 1884.
Age 44 years.

Charles Clark,
Born May 8, 1835.
Died Apr. 1, 1911.

(Douglass Graveyard p.2.)

Martha Brown Clark,
Born June 23, 1838.
Died Sept. 22,1912.

Charles B. Clark,
Born Apr. 27, 1875.
Died June 5, 1892.

Jennie M.,Wife of
Rev.R. K. Brown,
Born March 10, 1843.
Died Dec. 26,1862.

Benjamin D. Franklin,
Born Aug. 2, 1840.
Died Jan. 15,1862.

Bettie Looney, Wife of
Dr. P. Looney,
Born Feb. 26, 1832.
Died Sept. ----.

Here lies,
James R.D.Franklin,
Born Oct. 23, 1834.
Died Apr. 7, 1835.

Here lies the Remains of
William D. Franklin,
Born Apr. 23, 1829.
Died March --,1834.

Henry Franklin,
Born Aug. 23, 1826.

Peggy Green,Consort of
Lewis Green,
Born Dec.23, 1796.
Died Aug.20, 1828.

In Memory of
William Green,
Born Feb. 12, 1814.
Died June 20, 1850.

In Memory of
Thomas H. Bell,
Born Dec. 23, 1817.
Died Aug. 28, 1869.

SUMNER COUNTY

DOUGLASS
TOMBSTONE INSCRIPTIONS

Cemetery, located 5 miles on Douglass Pike north of Gallatin, Gallatin, Tennessee.
Copied by Mrs Alice Guthrie.

Louisa Douglass, consort of W.H.Douglass died Jan. 17,1821. Age 25 years.

A.H.Douglass died Sept. 9, 1855. Age 44 years.
"Death swallowed up in victory
Oh death where is thy sting
Oh grave where is thy victory
The sting of death is sin
And the strength of sin is the law
But thanks be to God who giveth up the victory."

James Douglass, born Mar.13, 1769. Died Mar. 29, 1837.

Catherine Douglass consort of James Douglass born Mar 29, 1771. Died Apr. 30, 1831. Married June 29, 1790.

Joseph Jenkins died Dec. 14, 1849. Age 27 years.

Robert George Douglass son of James & Catherine Douglass born Jan. 9, 1808. Died Sept. 27, 1844.

Elizabeth Douglass born Feb. __1807. Died Mar. 30, 18__.

M. Benetta Douglass born Sept. 28, 1813. Died Jan. 28, 1847.

Mrs Mary M.Murry, consort of Wm Murry, born Sept. 15, 1825. Died Feb. 16, 18__.

James D.Cook, born Dec. 20, 1822, died 1870.

Rev.Thomas L.Lyod, born Mar. 17, 1806. Died Nov. 12, 1847.

Young Norval, son of G.W.&L.E.Allen born Oct.6, 1858. Died June 13, 18___.

SUMNER COUNTY

DUNN
TOMBSTONE INSCRIPTIONS

Cemetery located on Canter farm 8½ miles from Gallatin, Tennessee.
Castalian Springs, Tennessee.
Copied by Mrs Alice Guthrie.

In memory of William Morgan son of Daniel R.Morgan born Aug. 14, 1839, died Jan. 31, 1840.

In memory Eliza R.Morgan consort of John E Morgan born May 10,1828, departed this life June 10, 1848.

Sarah Morgan consort of Chas Morgan born Dec. 23, 1792, died Apr.24, 1837.

Mary B Robb consort of Dr. E.C.Robb born Nov. 30, 1825, died Jan 15,1847.

Harley Holt born 1800, died 1853.

In memory of Elizabeth Thompson wife of B.W.Thompson was born the 1st day of April 1812. Died the 10th, of April 1858.

John Parrish born June 14,1819. Died May 10th, 1870.

To the memory of Charles Morgan born April 21, 1788. Died Mar. 29. 1860

TOMBSTONE - INSCRIPTIONS

EDWARDS GRAVEYARD
SUMNER COUNTY

Located in a Lot belonging to Mr. W. T. Goodall, 5½ miles West of Gallatin, Tenn., on Red River Road.
Copied by Mrs. Alice Guthrie, Gallatin, Tenn.
March 1, 1937.

"GINGY", Wife of
L. B. Edwards,
Born Aug. 27, 1793.
Died Nov. 5, 1878.
Age 85 years.

In Memory of
L. B. Edwards, Son of
Nathan Edwards,
"Jemia, his Wife",
Born in the State of
North Carolina, in the
County of Berte,
March 2, 1789.
Died Sept. 29, 1839.

(20 Field Stones.)

TOMBSTONE - INSCRIPTIONS

EDWARDS*LOVE GRAVEYARD
SUMNER COUNTY

Located in Lot of Mr. J. P. Kirk, 7 miles West of Gallatin, Tennessee, on Highway NO.25, Red River Road.
Copied by Mrs. Alice Guthrie, Gallatin, Tenn.
April 27, 1937.

Hiram Love,
Born May 16, 1812.
Died Aug. 17, 1860.

Charles Love, Son of
Hiram Love,
Born May --, 1846.
Died Aug. 16, 1888.

James Love, Son of
Hiram Love,
Born ----, 1840.
Died ----, 1882.

Mary Love,
Born Aug. 18, 1842.
Died May ---, 1865.

Julias E. Love,
Born Nov. 13, 1845.
Died May 9, 1848.

Thomas M. Cotton,
Born Sept. 27, 1848.
Died Mar. 5, 18--?

Patience Cotton, Wife of
Hugh Cotton,
Born June 4, 1802.
Died May 10, 1841.

Elizabeth Cotton,
Born July 18, 1852.
Died Sept. 15, 1855.

Sacred to the Memory of
Cullen Edwards,
Born March 31, 1796.
Died Aug. 17, 1815.

Nathan Edwards,
Born Mar. 27, 1755.
Died Feb. 21, 1837.

To the Memory of
Mrs. Jamima Edwards, Wife of
Nathan Edwards,
Born Jan. 11, 1762.
Died May 21, 1821.

Ann Eliza Edwards,
Born April 5, 1849.
Died Oct. 17, 1851.

William A. Edwards,
Born Aug. 23, 1813.
Died Dec. 27, 1844.

Priscilla Edwards,
Born Dec. 29, 1784.
Died May 16, 1848.

A Baptist of the Old
School, In Memory of
Thos. L. Edwards,
Born Aug. 20, 1782.
Died Mar. 12, 1849.

Almira Edwards,
Born Sept. 25, 1843.
Died June 8, 1857.
"Blessed are they that die in the Lord.

(Edwards Cemetery p. 2.)

Mary Elizabeth Price,
Born April 10, 1854,
Died Sept. 30, 1856.

Elizabeth Hunt, Daughter of
L. B. Edwards,
Born March 11, 1826.
Died -----,15, 1876.

Matilda, Wife of
Hugh George,
Born Aug. 23, 1815.
Died July 30, 1850.

Eliza J. George,
Born Feb. 3, 1847.
Died June 18, 1848.

William Hassell,
Born Jan. 22, 1818.
Died July 19, 1853.

(21 Inscriptions.)

SUMNER COUNTY

ELLIOTT

Tombstone Inscriptions

Cemetery located 9 miles on Dobbins Pike north of Gallatin. Old Elliott Home. Gallatin, Tennessee.
Copied by Mrs. Alice Guthrie.

In memory of Hugh Elliott born Oct. 3, 1837, died Aug. 21,1860.

Joseph McGee, Born Feb. 16, 1836, died Oct. 9, 1854.

James McGee, Born April 25, 1830, died Sept. 19, 1834.

Mary Jane wife of E.B.Rutledge born June 9, 1823, died June 2, 1860.
" A loving wife & devoted Mother."
Sometime in vision blessed, sweet spirit visit our repose and bear from thine own world of rest some balm for human woes what form more lovely could be given than thine, Oh messanger from heaven."

SUMNER COUNTY

FURGERSON
TOMBSTONE INSCRIPTIONS

Tombs, located in lot on Roscoe Home $2\frac{1}{2}$ miles Red River Road.
Gallatin, Tennessee.
Copied by Mrs Alice Guthrie.

Roxody Furgerson, Born Dec. 27, 1799, died Sept. 6, 1843.

Nelson Furgerson, born Jan. 25, 1793. Died May 8, 1825.

Blanch & Sally Loo. Blanch died July 11, 1858. Aged 15 mo. 28 days.
Sally Loo died 1858. 1 yr, daughters of Robert N. Miers & Cornelia A Miers.

SUMNER COUNTY

TOMBSTONE INSCRIPTIONS

Gallatin Cemetery, located in city of Gallatin.
Gallatin,Tennessee.
Copied by Mrs Alice Guthrie.

Woods Miller, born Dec. 5, 1809. Died Oct. 9, 1842.

In memory of Dr. N.B.Newson, born Feb. 11, 1822. Died Aug. 8, 1856.

Sacred to the memory of John Green Sims, born April 8, 1792. Died Aug. 22, 1824.

Sacred to the memory of Jesse Cage, born July 29, 1785. Died Aug. 8, 1846.

In memory of Gen. Zacheus Wilson who was born May 15, 1786. Died Nov 13, 1858.

To the memory of Wm H.Soloman born July 3, 1826. Died Apr. 16,1860.

Samuel W.Layderdale, born Apr. 18, 1844. Aged 22 years.

Nancy, wife of Maj. Wm Harvey born Sept. 8, 1796. Died Apr. 19, 1871.

William Harvey born Apr. 21, 1791. Died Feb. 24, 1862.

Sacred to the memory of Reuben Payne, born Apr. 2, 1781. Died Sept.18, 1836.

Charles Elliott, Died Sept.2, 1810. Age 35 years.

Elizabeth Elliston, consort of Joseph T.Elliston died Feb. 24,1846. Age 67 years 9 mo. & 10 days.

Rhoda Odom, -- 1817_age__.

Sacred to the memory of James Odom, Died June 6, 1825. Age 72 years.

Isaac Elliott, died Aug.16, 1825. Age 56 years.

Elijiah Boddie, born in Nash County North Carloina Sept. 8, 1787. Died in Sumner County Sept. 24, 1851.
"Mark the perfect man and behold the upright /
For the end of that man is peace."

SUMNER COUNTY

GLOVER
TOMBSTONE INSCRIPTIONS

Cemetery, located 2 miles east of Gallatin on Cairo Road.
Residence of Mrs Dell Barry, Gallatin,Tennessee.
Copied by Mrs Alice Guthrie.

Capt. Wm Glover, born Sept. 13, 1781. Died July 8, 1831.

I ____Glover born Apr. 18, 1814. Died July 12, 1830.

Catherine S Glover consort of William Glover born July 16, 1790, died Dec. 23, 1822.

SUMNER COUNTY

GREEN-CUMMINGS
TOMBSTONE INSCRIPTIONS

Cemetery, located 4½ miles west of Gallatin on Red River Pike.
Residence of Tom Cummings, Gallatin, Tennessee.
Copied by Mrs Alice Guthrie.

John W Green, born Jan. 12, 1812, died Aug. 6, 1876.
"Asleep in Jesus."

S.E.Cummings, born June 19, 1830. Died June 19, 1913.

Mrs S.E.Cummings, born June 15, 1836. Died June 12, 1913.
"Blessed are the dead which die in the Lord."

Edith Cummings, born Jan.9, 1803. Died Jan. 31, 1890.
" She is not dead but sleepeth."

SUMNER COUNTY

GREEN-FREEMAN
TOMBSTONE INSCRIPTIONS

Cemetery, located 4 miles Red River Road west of Gallatin.
Residence of Elmore Green, Gallatin, Tennessee.
Copied by Mrs Alice Guthrie.

Edward Green, born 1775. Died Apr. 3, 1880.

Mrs Edward Green born June 21, 1805. Died June 10, 1880.

Robert N. Miers born Sept. 26, 1813. Died Dec. 31, 1892.

Annie M. Green, born Feb. 14, 1842. Died Nov. 6, 1916.

Elmore H. Green born July 23, 1835. Died Jan. 5, 1884.
"Thy loving voice from which so of't
I consolution drew
No name I hear its tone so soft
My love one fond & true
Gone, but not, forgotten."

Blessed are they who die in the Lord. Sydna Bascom son of R.S.& J.G. Blankenship born Dec. 27, 1850. Died Nov. 20, 1874.
"Affection sore, long time I bore
Physician skill in vain
Till Christ was pleased to give me ease
And rid me of my pain."

Mary E. daughter of G.D.&S.A.Freeman born Aug. 30, 1871. Died Aug 4,1873.
"He ever lives above for me to intercede."

Richard Henry, son of G.D.&S.A.Freeman, born Sept 30, 1879. Died Aug.8,1880.
"Sleep on sweet Richard and take thy rest God called thee home when he thought best."

SUMNER COUNTY

HALL-HAYNES
TOMBSTONE INSCRIPTIONS

Cemetery, 10 miles from Gallatin, Tennessee.
In field of Charlie Smith, Castalian Springs, Tennessee.
Copied by Mrs Alice Guthrie.

Sacred to the memory of Katherine Hall, wife of Col. Wm.Hall born 1st, of June 1820. Died 2nd, April 1840.

Sacred to the memory of Robert P.Hall, son of William & Mary Hall born the twenty-eight of March A.D.1823. Died the 25th, of June A.D.1829. Age 6 years, 2 mo. & 27 days.

M.C.Hall daughter of W.H.& S.W.Hall born Sept 22, 1846, died Apr. 10, 1897. 1 mo.

W.H.Hall born Jan. 13, 1813. Died Oct. 29, 1883.
" He was indeed a Christian peace maker."

Lydia R.Winchester born Apr. 29, 1806. Was in early woman hood married to Winston McDaniel died Apr. 5, 1870. She died as she had lived Loved by all.

S.W.McDaniel born Jan. 8, 1828 married to W.H.Hall Sept. 1845. Died Feb. 26, 1882.
"Blessed are the dead who die in the Lord."
Erected by the children of W.H.& S.W.Hall.

In memory of Kate H.Barr daughter of J.W.& Katherine Hall wife of B.B.M.L. Ball born Dec. 27, 1839. Died Jan. 2, 1863.

Sacred to the memory of William Hall born the eleventh of February A.D. 1775. Died the seventh of October A.D.1856. Aged eighty one years seven months & twenty six days M.A.H.

In memory of Martha Ann Sharp, daughter of Gen. Wm and Mary Hall wife of Dr B.F.Sharp was born May 25, 1821. Died Oct. 4, 1852. Aged 31 years 4 months & 10 days.

Richard A.Hall born April 28, 1811. Died July 6, 1883.
"Blessed are the dead who die in the Lord."

Mammy Virginia T.Walsh, wife of Richard A.Hall born Dec. 8, 1825.Died May 8, 1912.
" Let her own words praise her in the gates."

John L.S.Haynes, born Oct. 21, 1835. Departed this life Jan. 23, 1840. Aged 5 years 3 mo. 82 days.
" Suffer little children to come unto me for such is the Kingdom of Heaven."

SUMNER COUNTY

HAMILTON-MALONE
TOMBSTONE INSCRIPTIONS

Cemetery, located 3 miles south of Gallatin.
Residence of J.W.Rankin, Gallatin,Tennessee.
Copied by Mrs Alice Guthrie.

Margaret Hamilton, wife of John Peyton born in Va Apr. 21,A.D.1768. Died in Sumner Co. Oct. 28,A.D.1812.

Lethe Eaton, daughter of S.W.&E.E.Malone, born Feb. 2, 1843.died July 19, 1865.

TOMBSTONE - INSCRIPTIONS

B. B. HARRIS CEMETERY
SUMNER COUNTY

State of Tennessee, County of Sumner, graves found in field o place owned by Mr. G. W. Carpenter Cotton Town, R.R.#1, ten miles west of Gallatin, Red River Road.
Alice Guthrie, Copyist, Gallatin, Tennessee.
June 8, 1937.

B. B. Harris, Born Jan. 6,
1791. Died Aug. 22, 1862.

Sally Harris, Born March 6,
1794. Died Jan. 6, 1863

Sarah, Wife of W. A. Gray,
Born July 31, 1837.
Died Feb. 9, 1879

SUMNER COUNTY

HENLEY
TOMBSTONE INSCRIPTIONS

Cemetery, located 3 miles west of Gallatin, on Red River Road.
Residence of J.E.Leath, Gallatin,Tennessee.
Copied by Mrs Alice Guthrie.

To the memory of John L.Henry born Jan.26, 1777. Died July 31, 1842.

In memory of Mrs Dorathy Henley, born Aug. 8, 1781. Died Sept. 20, 1820.

In memory of Henry B.Henley, born Apr. 6, 1814. Died Sept. 22, 1815.

In memory of Henrietta M Gaines born Feb. 12, 1852. Died Nov. 23, 1863.
" Of such is the Kingdom of Heaven."

In memory of Ann, wife of Jolm J.Henley born Aug. 23, 1795,died Oct. 2, 1859.
" Blessed are the dead which die in the Lord."

William Gaines, born Mar. 1, 1834. Died Feb.4, 1862.
" Blessed are they that die in the Lord."

Willie J Gaines, born May 26, 1861. Died May 31, 1861.
" Of such is the Kingdom of Heaven."

SUMNER COUNTY

HULLETT
TOMBSTONE INSCRIPTIONS

Private Cemetery located on Blythe Street 1 mile from Gallatin, Tenn.
Gallatin, Tennessee.
Copied by Mrs. Alice Guthrie. November 16, 1936.

Sarah, wife of L.Hullett, born Dec. 16, 1812, died Dec. 17,1876.

James Hullett, Born Sept. 2, 1841, died June 30, 1874.

124

SUMNER COUNTY

JOYNER
TOMBSTONE INSCRIPTIONS

Tombs located in field of James Summers 14 miles west of Gallatin on the Nashville, Pike near Hendersonville,Tenn.
Gallatin, Tennessee.
Copied by Mrs. Alice Guthrie.

Hugh Joyner, born Jan. 23,1805, died Oct. 19, 1885.

Annie Mills, born,1858, died 1892.

Lula

Cloe A.Bysor wife of R.W.Mills, born Aug. 10,1821 died Feb. 3,1908.

In memory of Sally E.Joyner wife of Hugh Joyner born Sept. 25,1799, died Apr. 27,1854.

To the memory of Nancy Davenport, born Oct. 14,1807, died Feb 8,1832.

Bennett, daughter of B.W.& C.A.Mills, born Mar 17,1850, died Aug.7,1850.

In memory of Dr. W.B.Davenport, Departed this life March 18,1842, aged about 60 years.

Peter Davenport, born 16, March 1826, Departed eartly life 14__..

Peter Bysor, born Nov. 19,1799, died Jan.1,1832.

William Davenport, born Dec. 28,1823, Died July 6,1825.

SUMNER COUNTY

KEARLEY
TOMBSTONE INSCRIPTIONS

Cemetery, located 4 miles on Hartsville Pike east of Gallatin.
Gallatin,Tennessee.
Copied by Mrs Alice Guthrie.

J.B.Kearley, born Dec. 5, 1819. Died Dec. 14, 1893.
" To forget is vain endeaver
Loves remembrance lasts forever."

Marthah, wife of J.B.Kearley born 1828. Died Jan. 29, 1882.
" Cherished in life, Tormented in death."

126

SUMNER COUNTY

KING
TOMBSTONE INSCRIPTIONS

Tombs located in field at the home of Mrs. Mattie Gray on Coles Ferry Pike 2 miles south of Gallatin.
Gallatin, Tennessee.
Copied by Mrs. Alice Guthrie. November 16, 1936.

In memory of Magadalane May, born Aug. 1796, died 1836.

Alfred L.H.Wallace, son of Herbert & Elizabeth Wallace born Feb. 21,1842, died Mar. 28,1848.

Here lies Bailey May, died Sept. 19,1828, age 36 years 6 months.

In memory of Alfred H.Wallace, born Jan. 6,1856, died Oct. 4,1857.

Erected to the memory of James Wilson, son of James & Sarah Wilson, born in Orange County North Carolina June 15,1788,died Aug. 7,1815.

A.B.Bruce, born Sept. 9,1851, died Sept. 1860.

To the memory of Rebecca Wallace, born May 1,1760, died Aug. 3,1851. Age 91 years.

Richard Alexander born May 10,1800, died July 26,1876.

Margaret Chapman, born Mar. 25,1798, died Nov. 11,1823.

Benjamin Chapman, born May 13,1789, died Dec. 4,1861.

Richard Bull, born Sept, 21, 1757, died Aug. 20, 1840.

Ann Anderson, wife of Richard Bull was born July 2, 1762, died June 4, 1841

James Pauling, son of Benjamin & Rebecca Chapman born May 31,1825, died Oct. 6,1848.

Rebecca Bull, wife of Benjamin Bull born July 11, 1802, died Jan. 9,1849.

In memory of Richard Blythe, born Dec. 23,1732 died July 9,1828.

Priscilla HASSELL Hi Hoene, formerly the consort of Wm. King died May 3,1822. Age 31 years.

Richard King, Age 66, died July 14,1824. 1834

Rachel B.King, Age 40 years. died Aug. 16,1815.

Mary King died May 1824. Age 66 years.

Anderson King, died Jan. 3,1831. Age 26 years.

Tombs located in Mrs.Mattie Grays Field,(Continued Page 2)

SUMNER COUNTY

TOMBSTONE INSCRIPTIONS

Elizabeth King, born Jan 10,1829, died Sept. 5,1845.

Nancy King, born Dec. 14,1803, died July 8,1841.

William Farr, died June 9, 1805.

Margaret Farr. Died June 2, 1803.

Martha K.Calhoun. Age 22 years died Apr. 6, 1822.

Nancy H.Blythe, born July 2,1812.

In memory of James Blythe died Dec. 1800. Age 65 years.

Christopher Daniel, born Mar. 18, 1820 died June 10,1849.

Jacob Rife, born Sept. 24,1791, died Apr. 27,1845.

35 Field stones.

SUMNER COUNTY

LAUDERDALE
TOMBSTONE INSCRIPTIONS

Cemetery, in field of Sam Harper 11 miles from Gallatin,Tenn.
Castalian Springs,Tennessee.
Copied by Mrs Alice Guthrie.

Thomas Kennedy M.D. born Mar. 13th 1827. Died Aug. 25, 1876.

Henry Head born Apr. 22, 1773.Died Feb. 8, 1852.

In memory of Providence Head consort of Pascal Head born Aug. 4, 1800, departed this life Oct. 5, 1837.

Dr. Henry Head, son of Pascal Head born May 7, 1827. Died Aug. 6, 1849.

William A Lauderdale born June 9, 1803. Died June 24, 1879.

In memory of Middleton Head, son of Henry Head born Aug. 18, 1802, died Sept. 16, 1825.

Joseph Robb, Infant son of J.Y.& Clara Robb born Mar. 20, 1862. Died 1862.

Sacred to the memory of Dr. Leonadus Johnson born May 9, 1834. Died June 15, 1865.

In memory of Benjamin Head, son of Bevely & Eveline Head born May____ Died Jan. 6, 1843. Age 7 mo.

Evelyn Head consort of Henry Head born June 15, 1777. Died Apr. 4, 1878.

Penelope E, daughter of Pascal & Providence Head born June 6, 1831. departed this life 1835.

Lucy Marian, daughter of Henry & Evelyn Head died Mar. 4, 1841 aged 2 years.

Evelina, wife of B.Head born Feb. 21, 1816. Died ________

Raymond B.Head born May 14, 1838. Died Apr. 7, 1858.

In memory of Beverly Head, born Nov 2, 1808. Died Oct. 2nd.

In memory of Lucy Johnson consort of Matthew Johnson born Mar.31, 1800, died Oct. 2, 1840.

Sacred to the memory of Dr Nimrod B Johnson born June 23, 1836.

SUMNER COUNTY

RAWLINGS
TOMBSTONE INSCRIPTIONS

Cemetery, located 6 miles on Long Hollow Pike.
Residence of Dodson Home Gallatin,Tennessee.
Copied by Mrs Alice Guthrie.

To the memory of Margarett T.Watkins, daughter of Benjamin Rawlings born Oct. 11, 1802. Died Jan. 22, 1828.

"Cut off untimely in lifes tender bloom
Thy memory long shall deep affection prize
And said remembrance haunt this hallowed tomb
Where, truth & worth & moral beauty lies."

To the memory of Miss Laetitia Rawlings 18 of ___1824 age 19 years.

(130)

TOMBSTONE - INSCRIPTIONS

RICE-HENLY GRAVEYARD
SUMNER COUNTY

Located in a Field owned by Mr. Erskine Turner, 2½ miles East of Gallatin, Tenn., on the Scottsville Pike. There are 18 un-marked graves, and 8 marked graves. Copied by Mrs. Alice Guthrie, Gallatin, Tennessee. April 23, 1937.

Julia W. Rice, Wife of
Dr. C. A. Rice, Daughter of
J.M. & Mary Rice, Was lost on t
The ill-fated Steamer-W.H.Carter,
Feb. 2, 1866.

Mary Ann Henly,
Born ---, 1800.
Departed this life
July 10, ----?

In Memory of
John Martin Henly,
Born Nov. 1801.

Dr. Thomas Donnell,
Died Feb. 8, 1842.
Age 86 years.

Mary Jane Donnell, Consort of
Robert Donnell,
Died Nov. 14, 1836.
Age 19 years.

Robert K. Donnell,
Died March 13, 1821.
Age 26 years.

Mrs. Nancy Bain,
Departed this life,
April 1829.

John Purviance,
Age 24 years-Fell by
Indian Barbarity.
May 7, 1792.

SUMNER COUNTY

ROBB
TOMBSTONE INSCRIPTIONS

Cemetery, located 2 miles from square of Gallatin,Tennessee.
Residence of Mrs S.W.Whitaker, Hartsville Pike, Gallatin.
Copied by Mrs Alice Guthrie.

In memory of Anna Robb, consort of Joseph Robb who departed this life July 3rd 1846 in the 56th year of her age.
Thou art gone gone to the grave
We no longer behold <u>three</u>.

To the memory of Robert Hodge, who departed this life on the 7th of July 1847, aged 57 years.

Sacred to the memory of Joel Parrish, who departed this life on the 14th day of September 1859, aged 76 years.

To the memory of Mrs Jane Hodge, wife of Robert Hodge and mother of two surviving children was born 24th, March 1793 and departed this life 8th Feby 1829.

To memory of Joseph Robb, born April 11, 1781, died Nov. 11, 1861.
The steps of a good man are ordered by the Lord.

William Glover Jr, born April 13th 1818 and departed this life Sept'r next ensueing.

An infants grave next to William Robb Sr.

William Robb Sr, departed this life 1st January 1830 was born 2nd March 1761.
"By long experience have I known thy sovereign power to to save at thy command I venture down safety to the grave. When I die buried deep in dust My flesh shall be thy care The withering limbs with thee I trust to raise them strong and fair.

H.T.Stewart, born June 15, 1790, aged 12 years.

John Sloss died on the 29th April 1313 or 1818, aged 23 years.
" Let us be warn'd from all below
Let hope on light of gospel
Here lies the body of

Here lies the body of Sarah Hudson, who departed this life April 30th, 1826 in the 60th year of her age.
" Alas sh's gone from earth afar
She left these scenes of toil
And care, Of blessed fruits to reap her share in heaven
Lord unto this affliction blow, with Calm submission may she bow,
And like our friend prepare to go to heaven".

Here lies the body of Joseph Motheral, born May 5th, 17_9. Departed this life _28, 1316.

SUMNER COUNTY

Robert Foster was born April the twenty fifth 1787, and departed this life Feb. 9, 1806 in the 18th year of his age.

"To youthful bloom death laid me down here to wait the trumpets sound
Prepare for death while you have time
For I was taken in my prime."

Sacred to the memory of Elizabeth Glover consort of W.I.L.L.I.A.M. Glover who died________

Our Mother Harriett M.Hodges wife of James M.Bryson born Feb 1, 1819, died June 20, 1877.

Our father James M Bryson, born March 12, 1811, died July 20, 1884.

Our father Richard Alexander, born Aug. 21, 1843, died May 10, 1888.

Mary E King born Aug. 14, 1828, died July 3rd, 1847.

To the memory of Mrs Jane M Blackmore wife of J.A.Blackmore, she was born March 27, 1821 and died March 29th, 1856. Aged 35 years and 2 days.

TOMBSTONE - INSCRIPTIONS

ROBERTS-RIGGSBEE
SUMNER COUNTY

These tombs were found in a field belonging to Mrs. James Conyer, 11 miles west of Gallatin, on Red River Road.
This Cemetery had no name.
Copied by Alice Baker Gutherie, Sumner, County, Tennessee
July 23, 1937

Mattie Ann
Wife of
J. H. Roberts
Born November 2, 1867
Died November 29, 1897
"Gone but not Forgotten"

Jeff Riggsbee
Born February 20, 1866
Died November 11, 1928

Six Field Stones.

(134)

SUMNER COUNTY

SANDERS
TOMBSTONE INSCRIPTIONS

Tombs located in field of Mrs. Horatio Berrys farm 18 miles west of Gallatin on Walton's Ferry Road near Hendersonville, Tennessee. Gallatin, Tennessee.
Copied by Mrs. Alice Guthrie

In memory of Franklin Sanders, son of James & Hannah Sanders.

Mary Sanders, born April 26,1781 died Dec. 29, 1857. Daughter of General Dan Smith first married to Samuel Donelson then to James Sanders.
"She was in deed a mother in Isreal
Lived & died a Christian."

James Sanders Esq., born in North Carolina Oct.31,1761, died in Sumner County Aug. 4,1836.

Giles Jones, born Ded. 17 1810, died July 17,1869.

In memory of Martha Watson, consort of Dr. Thorn Ten Watson, born March 17,1811, died Feb. 5, 1860.

To the memory of Hannah Sanders, daughter of James Sanders & Hannah Sanders.

This slab is dedicated to the memory of James Sanders Esq., who was born in N.C. 31, Oct. 1764, died in Sumner County Tennessee on the 24th ? Aug. 1836.
" He was a good husband, a kind parent, an honest man, he enjoyed the confidence of his neighbor.
He loved virtue for its own sake & hated vice for its deformity.
There was none more ready to do a good act or condemned a mean one,
Peace be to his ashes."

SUMNER COUNTY

SAUNDERS
TOMBSTONE INSCRIPTIONS

Tombs located in field of farm known as the Old Saunders home, 10 miles west of Gallatin on the Nashville Pike near Hendersonville,Tenn. Gallatin, Tennessee.
Copied by Mrs. Alice Guthrie.

Sacred to the family of H.H. & E.M.Saunders.

Rev. Hubbard Saunders, died 1829 age about 64 years.

Chloe wife of Hubbard Saunders died 1850, age about 74 years.

William B.Saunders, born 1849 died 1928.

Maggie D.Saunders, born 1871 died 1905.

Robert E.Saunders born 1859, died 1925.

Lizzie Saunders, born 1871 died 1887.

Hubbard H.Saunders, born 1819 died 1879.

Elizabeth B.Saunders, born 1828 died 1906.

Madison Martin, born Nov. 22 1813 died Aug. 5 1862.
"Once a pilgrim once a stranger,
Now an angel and a blessed child of light."

In memory of Hubbard Wilkins M.D. son of Robert & Nancy A.Harper, died Oct. 28,1856 aged 23 years.

In memory of Nancy A.Harper wife of Robt. Harper Born in 1793, died Nov. 11, 1857 aged 64 years.

In memory of Robert Harper born in Dinwiddie County Va Jan. 27,1785, died Oct. 23,1866.
"I Know that my redeemer liveth."

John Green, died June 2,1864 aged about 36 years.

In memory of John A.Walker born Dec.9,1790 died Aug 15,1861.

In memory of Mrs. Elizabeth Walker, born Sept. 8 1795, departed this life Sept. 16 1840.
"In the full triumph of a living faith and beloved by all her acquaintances.

In memory of John H.Read, born Feb.14,1825 died Nov. 22,1836.

In memory of A.E.Duncan, born 1826 died July 1851.

SUMNER COUNTY

Tombstone Inscriptions SHELBY

Cemetery located in lot at Spencers Choice, home now owned by Mr.Johnson, South Water St. Gallatin, Tennessee.
Copied by Mrs Alice Guthrie.

Sacred to the memory of D-vid Shelby Esq. born Sept. 12, 1822, 60 years of age.

Infant daughter of David Shelby born July 15, 1801, died Aug. 2, 1805.

Priscilla Douglass born Mar. 8, 1793, Died ___13, 1815.

137

SUMNER COUNTY

SHELBY
TOMBSTONE INSCRIPTIONS

Cemetery, located 3 miles north of Gallatin on Dobbins Pike.
Field of Walter Elliott, Gallatin, Tennessee.
Copied by Mrs Alice Guthrie.

In memory of Mrs Albert Shelby, departed this life Apr. 16, 1829 in the 21st year of herlife. 12 months & 4 days after her marriage.

"From Deaths cold touch that lays earthly glories low
No charm of beauty of worth can save
The rich, the poor alike sustain the blow
That brings thee prospects to an earthly grave
Let hope survive the sad and solumn scene
And points to realms and happiness on high
Where neither__nor darkness in ___
To blight out joys or heave misfortunes sigh."

Auslem B.Holmes, died July 26, 1822. Age 22 years 3 mo. 29 days.

Mrs Mary Wright died July 13, 1822. Age 24 years.

Nancy Lewis, wife of Charles Lewis died Mar 24, 1857. age 60 years.
" Here sleep in dust the Almighty will then rise unchanged and be an angel still.

Charles Lewis, age 46 years died Dec. 1812.

Mrs Frances Smith, Died July 2, 1831. Age 29 years.

In memory of Anne Bugg, born Sept. 22, 1791. Died Mar. 2, 1816.

Frances Bugg, born Mar. 3, 1772. Died Jan.18, 1835.

Belvidera Adelaide Trousdale, born Apr. 6, 1833. Died Sept. 19, 1833. Age 5 mo.

In memory of Sam'l Bugg born Feb. 16, 1762. Died Feb. 23, 1816.

To the memory of Joyce Alexander Bugg, born May 30, 1815. Married July 27, 1835. Died July 18, 1844. Age 29 years.

A.D.Bugg, born Feb. 23, 1794. Died Jan. 1849.

Emly Donelson Bugg, born March 19,___Died July 6, 1835.

Walter L.Bugg, born May 30, 1815. died July 18, 1844. Married July 27, 1845.

Gyrus Wilson Dodd, born Feb. 6, 1836. Died Nov. 11, 1860.

William Dodd, born Dec. 19, 1913.

Weaver b. 7/1781 d. 7/22/1845
Joe born July 1781 died July 22.1845.

138

Tombstone Insdriptions SHILO

Cemetery located at Shilo Church 5 miles east of Gallatin
Gallatin, Tennessee.
Copied by Mrs Alice Guthrie.

Amanda Franklin, born Apr. 21, 1823, died Jan. 25, 1887.

J.J.Franklin, born Sept. 15, 1847, died Aug.18,1912.

Emely J.Franklin, Born Dec. 26, 1847, died Jan. 19,1919.

SUMNER COUNTY

SHOULDERS
TOMBSTONE INSCRIPTIONS

Cemetery, 3 miles west of Gallatin, on Red River Road.
Residence of J.B.Pardue, Gallatin,Tennessee.
Copied by Mrs Alice Guthrie.

Thomas Sholdis, born Jan. 13, 1804. Died Sept. 9, 1824.

Here is the boddie of Mrs Thomas Sholdiers, born Sept. 9, 1787. Died Oct. 2, 1823.

SUMNER COUNTY

SMITH
TOMBSTONE INSCRIPTIONS

Tombs located on farm of Mrs. Horatio Berry, at the Old Rock house on the Indian Lake road,near Hendersonville Tenn on Nashville Pike. Gallatin,Tennessee.
Copied by Mrs. Alice Guthrie.

Harry Smith born Oct. 19,1806, died July 16,1888.

Sallie E. wife of H.S.Smith, born Jan.2,1837, died Oct.29,1863.

Tabitha, daughter of H.& S.E.Smith, born June 4,1863, died Oct. 15,1872.

In memory of Tabitha Bugg, daughter ofCol. George & Tabitha Smith wife of Anslem D.Bugg, born Nov. 13,1803, died Sept. 18,1869.

In memory of Col. Geo. Smith, born May 12,1776, died Feb. 15,1849.

Gen. Daniel Smith, born Oct. 29,1743, died June 16,1815.

Sarah Smith, born Jan. 30,1755, died Apr. 2,1834.

Alfred Smith died Aug. 16,1886, age 71 years.

Easter Smith died Feb. 17,1884 age 57 years.

William Murray, born Oct. 4,1823, died Aug 18,1883.

Armfield Murray, born Aug. 15,1862, died Mar.5,1901.

Mary Bugg, wife of William Murray born June 15,1828, died Sept. 1, 1872.

Samuel Bugg born Sept. 1823, died Nov. 25,1899.

John J.Wherry, born June 19,1817, died November 14,1875.

William Wherry, born April 18,1854, died July 17,1863.

Mary J.Wherry, born Feb. 19,1856, died July 28, 1863.

Emily Johnson Wherry, born July 24,1858, died Aug.4,1863.

John M.Wherry, born Mar. 2,1841, died Oct. 8th 1862. At Perryville,Ky.

Daniel S.Wherry, born Sept.8,1845, died Aug. 21,1846.

Evelyn A.Wherry, born Mar. 12,1843, died Oct. 21,1846.

Augusta K.Wherry, wife of W.D.Hamilton, born Dec. 14,1858, died July 28,1897.

SUMNER COUNTY

SOPER
TOMBSTONE INSCRIPTIONS

Tombs located in field of Miss Bessie Soper 2 miles on Coles Ferry Pike south of Gallatin, Tennessee Sumner county.
Gallatin,Tennessee.
Copied by Mrs.'Alice Guthrie. November 16, 1936.

Rebecca Gourley, born Feb. 1,1818, died Aug. 4,1892.
" Rest Mother rest in quiet sleep
While friends in sorrow over thee weep."

Samuel Gourley, born Aug. 4,1816, died Feb. 21,1866.

David Gourley, born Dec. 12,1850, died Nov. 18,1852.

James A.Soper, born Mar. 15,1843, died June 29,1925.

Malisa C.Ophella, wife of Jas. A.Soper born Oct. 25,1848, died Jan. 31,1877.

Mary E.Soper, born Oct. 24,1856, died Feb.13,1895.

Maudie E.Soper, born Nov. 5,1875, died Jan. 18,1893.

Joseph S.Denny, born Nov. 8,1884, died July 28,1892.

12 Field Stones.

SUMNER COUNTY

Tombstone Inscriptions SOPER

Cemetery, located in lot on place known as Wade Andersons farm 7 miles west Gallatin, Tennessee on Cages Bend road.
Copied by Mrs. Alice Guthrie

In memory of John Soper, born Nov. 25,1794, died Nov.17, 1866.

To the memory of Mary J.Soper, who was born Feb. 5, 1794, died Feb.6,1852.

SUMNER COUNTY

STINSON
TOMBSTONE INSCRIPTIONS

Tomb, in field of William Bate, 9 miles on Hartsville Pike from Gallatin Castalian, Springs, Tennessee.
Copied by Mrs Alice Guthrie.

Garble Nettie Stinson born Aug. 4, 1887. Died Jan. 20, 1910.

TOMBSTONE - INSCRIPTIONS

STONE
SUMNER COUNTY

Tomb located in Field of place owned by Mr. Frank Gillespie, 6½ miles West of Gallatin, Tenn. on Highway NO.25, Red River Road.
Copied by Mrs. Alice Guthrie, Gallatin, Tenn.
April 27, 1937.

William Stone,
Born ----, 1784.
Died April 18, 1840.

25 Field Stones.
1 Inscription.

SUMNER COUNTY

SUDDARTH
TOMBSTONE INSCRIPTIONS

Tombs located in field of Mrs. James Suddarth on Coles Ferry Pike
2 miles south of Gallatin Sumner County
Gallatin, Tennessee
Copied by Mrs. Alice Guthrie. November 16, 1936.

James Suddarth, died Aug. 27,1933. Age 65 years.

Field Stones - 5.

SUMNER COUNTY

TROUSDALE
TOMBSTONE INSCRIPTIONS

CEMETERY, located in yard of old Trousdale place owned by K.B.Dunklin.
Residence North Water St, Gallatin, Tennessee.
Copied by Mrs Alice Guthrie.

Capt. James Trousdale died 24th of Dec. 1818, age 82 years.

SUMNER COUNTY

VINSON
TOMBSTONE INSCRIPTIONS

Tombs located in field of farm owned by Jim Franklin, Coles Ferry Pike 4½ miles south of Gallatin.
Gallatin, Tennessee.
Copied by Mrs. Alice Guthrie - November 16, 1936.

Capt. James Vinson, born May 20,1764, died May 11,1822.

To the memory of Charity Vinson wife of Enos Vinson, born Mar. 20, 1792, died May 15,1829.

Thomas Vinson, born July 1,1833, died Sept. 1861.

Turner B.Vinson, born July 10,1815, died July 20,1855.

William Vinson, born Dec. 11,1812, died June 17,1840.

Rhoda Vinson, consort of Capt. James Vinson, born July 8, 1761, died Aug. 11,1856.

6 Field Stones.

SUMNER COUNTY

Tombstone Inscriptions WALLACE

Cemetery located in lot of Old Wallace place 8 miles north of Gallatin on Dobbins pike ½ mile left. Gallatin, Tennessee.
Copied by Mrs. Alice Guthrie.

Joseph B.Wallace, born Oct. 16, 1819, died June 26, 1862.

Julias Wallace, son of J.B.& S.A.Wallace born Nov. 26, 1846, died May 19, 1869.

TOMBSTONE - INSCRIPTIONS

WALTON GRAVEYARD
SUMNER COUNTY

Located 9½ miles West of Gallatin, Tennessee, on Station Camp Creek Road, in a field on place owned by Mrs. Mary Ann Mitchell.
Copied by Mrs. Alice Guthrie, Gallatin, Tennessee.
April 8, 1937.

Eugene Walton,
Born Aug. 28, 1865.
Died June 22, 1874.

William J. Walton,
Born Dec. 19, 1851.
Died Nov. 7, 1872.

In Memory of
Mrs. Sally Walton,
Born July 12, 1792.
Died April 10, 1876.

Josiah Walton,
Born Aug. 6, 1788.
Died Aug. 5, 1857.
" Let me die the death of
the rightious, Let my
last be like His."

In Memory of
Sabeler G. McKain, Wife of
Eli G. McKain,
Born May 24, 1814.
Died Sept. 1, 1853.

In Memory of
Cynthia G. Walton,
Born March 23, 1833.
Died June 14, 1850.

In Memory of
Amanda Walton,
Born Oct. ---, 1824.
Died July 31, 1844.

Sabella McKain,
Born May 8, 1857.
Died March 20, 1866.

Josiah McKain,
Born Dec. 5, 1838.
Died Apr. 4, 1883.

Mat McKain,
Born Sept. 9, 1835.
Died Nov. 3, 1928.

OUR FATHER:
G. A. Kirk,
Born Sept. 11, 1838.
Died Feb. 14, 1894.

John G. McKain,
Born March 22, 1839.
Died April 8, 1917.

Eli, Son of
E.G. & S.O. McKain,
Born July 10, 1853.
Died Sept. 4, 1857.

Lizzie Young,
Born Feb. 18, 1838.
Died April 18, 1906.
Ann McKain,
Born May 28, 1842.
Died Jan. 28, 1914.

James W. Walker,
Died Aug. 11, 1876.
"Blessed are the dead,
Who die in the Lord."

(Walton Graveyard p.2.)

Amanda Louise Kirk,
Born Dec. 1, 1846.
Died July 11, 1920.

(There are 2 Field Stones.)

151

SUMNER COUNTY

WEATHERRED
TOMBSTONE INSCRIPTIONS

Cemetery, 9 miles from Gallatin,Tennessee on Hartsville Pike in lot near Residence of Frank Chenault Castalian Springs, Tennessee.
Copied by Mrs Alice Guthrie.

In memory of William Weatherred born Oct. 6, 1779. Departed this life 28th of May 1849.

In meomory of Sarah C Bush daughter of Hezekiah & Nancy Lyon born Nov.26, 1806. Died Mar. 8, 1851.

Mrs Weatherred 1849.

SUMNER COUNTY

152

WILLIS
TOMBSTONE INSCRIPTIONS

Tombs located in field of Miss Sarah Berry's farm about 12 miles west of Gallatin on the Nashville Pike, near Hendersonville, Tenn.
Gallatin, Tennessee.
Copied by Mrs. Alice Guthrie.

Stephen G.Willis, died March 19, 1881, aged 61 years 7 Mos.4 Ds.

Mary Sophia, wife of Stephen Willis, born July 1827 died Aug. 30,1872.

Jane Willis born Feb. 8, 1859 died Sept. 2, 1865.

William E.Willis, born Dec. 24,1854 died Sept. 22.1857, 4 yrs.-8Mo.-28 days.

Lizzie Willis, born July 9, 1861, died Sept. 9, 1865.

Sallie G.Willis born Mar. 12,1857, died Sept. 5,1865.

Priestly Bradford, born Feb. 7,1795, died May 7,1854.

Elizabeth Jonette, wife of P.Bradford born Mar.26,1799,died Sept.14, 1855.

Norman Bradford born Mar. 14,1826, died Apr. 11,1854.

Cecilia Bradford born Dec. 27,1830 died Aug 1,1849.

Jane D.Arlington, 4 field stones.

SUMNER COUNTY

WILSON
TOMBSTONE INSCRIPTIONS

Cemetery, located 3 miles on Dobbins Pike north of Gallatin.
In field on farm of Jim Hix, Gallatin, Tennessee.
Copied by Mrs Alice Guthrie.

Sacred to the memory of Samuel Wilson, died Aug. 11, 1849. Age 50 years.

This is to the memory of Anna Wilson, born May 6, 1759. Died Aug.9,1840.

This is to the memory of John Wilson, born Dec. 27, 1759. Died Oct.28, 1856. 1836

SUMNER COUNTY

WINCHESTER
TOMBSTONE INSCRIPTIONS

Cemetery located on "Cragfont Farm" 7½ miles on Hartsville Pike.
Gallatin, Tennessee.
Copied by Mrs Alice Guthrie.

General James Winchester, born 1752, died 1826. Captain in Maryland line American Revolution. Pioneer settler of Sumner county Tennessee, Brigadier General U.S.A. in command of left wing of the north west 1812-1813. On command at Nashville 1814-1815. First speaker of the State Senate 1796. Commissioner as to Chickasaw boundary line 1819 one of the founders of Memphis, friend of Jackson and Overton and being a leading citizen of Tennessee.

"How of't alas we see the worthless name bedecked by fraud with trophies of the brave.

While lost, forgotten or unknown fame, oblivious wings obscures the patriots grave, but when faulse claims to glory meet their doom, and truth with clarion note once more shall Rise

The historic muse will point to this lone tomb.
Where native worth and spotless honor lies."

Chas Cassedy.

Susan Black Winchester 1777-1864.

Helen Mae Winchester 1813-1880.

In memory of Major Geo Winchester who was ______________

Almira Winchester Wynne 1808-1883.

Col. Alfred R.Wynne 1800-1893.

Joseph Guild Wynne 1848-1887.

Elizabeth Carloine Shelby wife of Orville Shelby and daughter of James Winchester, was born on the 10th Jan. 1802. Departed this life on the 25th, October 1827.

" If these rare virtues of her possessed
With charms impart to all of worth in life."

Sacred to the memory of Caroline E Wynne born Jan. 17, 1831, died Dec.21, 1854.

" Tis vain to weep 'tis vain to sigh
Tis vain this idle speech
For where her happy soul doth lie
Our fear will never reach."

Louisa Winchester Rucker 1810-1888.

In memory of Robert Wynn who was born the 19th of Feb. 1827.
" As brave and noble a heart as ever beat in mortal breast was stilled in death by the hand of an assin on the 31st day of July 1860." May he rest in peace.

In memory of William Hall Wynn born Nov. 18, 1843, died June 24, 1862. "Far from his home in obedience to the call of his country he offered up his young life in the hope of a happy resurrection."

TOMBSTONE - INSCRIPTIONS

WOLF HILL CEMETERY
SUMNER COUNTY

This Cemetery is located 15 miles East of Gallatin on Jackson Highway 31-E.
Copied by Alice Baker Gutherie, Summer County, Tennessee
July 23, 1937

Elizabeth Crews
Born January 1, 1833
Died January 17, 1909

Lula Crews
Born December 24, 1907
Died November 19, 1934

Mrs. J. W. Crews
Born July 9, 1880
Died August 8, 1935

A. F. Thurman
Born March 8, 1861
Died November 27, 1915

Nellie Gaines Carr
Born February 18, 1920
Died March 27, 1890

Lizzie Gaines
Born October 30, 1873
Died January 31, 1914

J. L. Reed
Born June 2, 1880
Died May 31, 1934

Jim Reed
Born June 26, 1851
Died March 24, 1934

SUMNER COUNTY

CIVIL WAR RECORD
MARY J. GARDNER PASS

The following record is a copy of the original pass issued by the Provost Marshal to Miss Mary J. Gardner, a daughter of Cullen Bryant Gardner, and the mother of Mrs. Walter Love of West Main St., Gallatin, Tennessee. This pass, granted by the Union Army, permitted Miss Gardner to go within the Federal lines, and is at present time owned by Mrs. Walter Love of Sumner County, who lives on West Main St., Gallatin, Tennessee.

Copied by Mrs. Alice Baker Guthrie, Gallatin, Tennessee - October 1938.

Provost Marshals office
Gallatin, Tenn.
Nov. 29 - 1864.

Guards & pickets,

Pass - Miss Mary J. Gardner

for 30 days within Federal lines by order of

James Gilfillan
Col. 11th. Minn. Inft.
Commanding post.

A. R. Hall, 1st. Lieut. Minn. Inft.
Provost Marshal

* * * * *

CIVIL WAR LETTER
J. C. HURMANS TO DR. P. W. DUNCAN

The following letter is a copy of the original letter written from Camp by J. C. Hurmans, a confederate soldier, to Dr. P. W. Duncan, as it was almost impossible to get a letter to his parents, Mr. & Mrs. Sylvanus Hurmans. The letter is owned at the present time by a neice of J. C. Hurmans, Miss Annie Brown of North Water St., Gallatin, Tennessee.

Copied by Mrs. Alice Baker Guthrie, Gallatin, Tennessee - September 16, 1938.

Camp Butler,
Sangamom Co. Ill.,

Dr. P. W. Duncan.

Sir:

I attempt adressing you, though I guess it will be quite unexpected to you, yet as I suppose you would like to know where ___ are and what has become of the Ft. Donelson Prisoners I can assure you we have well experienced the toils of war, as our forefathers, also the life of a prisiner of war, which of all is the most trying to the heart of man. Though a prisoner, amid the enemy we are regarded as human & as a people of feeling, both morally, intellectually & politically, we find them friendly and kind whither we go. No doubt but what we have been misled to some extent. I have been reading daily papers very close since I've been here, besides I have had various conversations with them, some very eloquent, well posted apparently, our situation is quite a nice one, we have splendid barracks, 100 men to the Barrack. rather too many for health & the water does not agree with us, that with the brutely exposure before leaving, a great deal pneumonia, fever & diaphria. We lay behind the parapets in ditches amid the mud, snow & rain four days & nights in succession without proper raiment, eating nothing during the day, could cook only during the night, exposed to the snow & rain intolerable. All went off well until those horrible bumshells from six to sixty four, or eighty four balls, like six horse wagon bubs, those wave from the boat on the opposite side of us, on a hill was placed a small battery, throwing shot & shell where ever a man would step out the pits.

We were in the fight on the right wing Saturday, though lost no men out of our Company. Capt. Buntin lost one man & himself wounded in the thigh (flesh wound). Our Col. left us Saturday night. I would have been glad, but they have caught him while shabbing. He had been wanting to leave us from the time they commenced landing troops at Smithland. Our commissioned officers are all taken from, no I suppose they are at St. Louis. We are about five miles east of Springfield, Ill. and the Springfield & Chicago railroad.

We have lost no man yet, unless it be Ted Phenix & Cris Huffines, they were missing Saturday, suppose they fled for home. We all have

very bad colds & coughs, nothing more at present.
You will give my best wishes & respect to all.
Please hand this to Pa after reading.

Remain as ever,

J. C. Hurmans

P. S.
You will please write soon and let me know the state of affairs in Kentucky and Tennessee, and how the health of all my friends.

J. C. H.

* * *

Mrs. Hurmans:

I was as much surprised as pleased to receive this letter.
Allow me to congratulate you upon his good health and fine spirits. May the time not be long before you may have the pleasure of embracing your darling boy.

Resp't.

G. W. Duncan.

* * * * *

CIVIL WAR LETTER
GEN. JOHN H. MORGAN TO COL. THOS. BOYERS

The following letter is a copy of the original one written by General John H. Morgan to Col. Thos. Boyers, concerning his stepson, Jack Brown. The letter is at present owned by Mrs. Annie Boyers Baker, Gallatin, Tennessee, Sumner County, who is a half sister of Jack Brown, and daughter of Col. Boyers.

Col. Thos. Boyers' second wife, Annie Boyers, first married a Brown, having two sons, Jack & Billy. Jack was only 13 years old when he enlisted with the Confederate Army. As the troops were passing through Gallatin he ran away with them, riding on a horse behind Gen. John Morgan. Jack Brown was very young at the time he enlisted, but very brave, and fought bravely in the war between the States, ranking as a Captain.

Copied by Mrs. Alice Baker Guthrie, Gallatin, Tennessee - October 6, 1938.

McMinnville
April 20, 1863

Col. Boyers.

Dear Col.

Jack arrived last Saturday, is well, in fact looks better than I ever saw him, has grown a great deal.

He is not willing to leave here.

Give my regards to your lady.

Yours truly,

John H. Morgan.

* * * * *

SUMNER COUNTY

CIVIL WAR LETTER
CHARLEY W. OWEN TO MR. GARDNER

The following letter is a copy of the original one written from Camp Winchester by Charley W. Owen, a Confederate Soldier, to a friend, Mr. Gardner. This letter is at the present time owned by Mrs. Walter Love, Gallatin, Tennessee, Sumner County, a granddaughter of Mr.Gardner. Mrs. Love's mother, Mrs. Mollie Herring was a daughter of Mr. Gardner, and her great grandmother was a very near relative of Robt. E. Lee.

Copied by Mrs. Alice Baker Guthrie, Gallatin, Tennessee - October 1938.

Camp Winchester
Aug. the 13th. 1861

Mr. Gardner.

Sir:

As this is the first oppertunity that I ever had to write to you I thought I would try to write to you a line or two to let you know how we are all getting along. We are a doing very well under the surrounding circumstances. We are in Camp about two miles from Potomac River, and about twenty five miles from Fredericksburg, and about forty miles from Washington City.

Well I have nothing to write to you of interest only we are all in tolerable good health, thare several of our Company sick, the desease are generally chills and fever and some few cases of billious fever, though none very serious. I have been sick myself, but I have got well again. William T. House has been quite sick, but I heard yesterday he was better. He is in Fredicksburg at a private house, so he is treated with great kindness and attention that could be paid him. The people of that City are very kind and hospital indeed.

I reckon you have heard of the battle of Manasas Gap, that was one of the greatest battles that was recorded on any History whatever there is. I saw many dead and wounded men, there were legs and arms, and I saw one poor fellow with his head blown off down to his neck and only left a part of his whiskers on the skin. He was a yankee, but he is a yankee no more, and I saw another Yankee, his mouth and teeth were all blown out and _________ you _______ to eat the Southern bread no more.

Well, the crops look very well here, though nothing to compare with the Tennessee crops. They made very good wheat on crops for the soil it had to grow on here, very thin, somewhat like that over the ridge.

Mr. Gardner you just ought to be here to go with the ladies to church. When they get ready to go to church they order their ox and hitch him to a cart and generally four women and two old men get in and go in double quick time three or four miles. The carts are made on the plans of a drag, they can take out the pen that holds the bed together and then the driver will raise up the far end of the bed and they will slip out and after preaching they will hitch up and go like the _____ down grade, that is most of that.

Captain Tyree is well and fat, he is a good Captain to his men.

Well I will tell you something about the cannon balls and boom-shells, they fell like hail for some two hours. We were ordered on the battle ground, but when the Yankees saw us coming they retreated in double quick time, they could not stand the sight of the Walkers session. You know they would have fought like Turks. I will now tell you something about how we cook. We have got to be excellent cooks. We get up in the morning and make our fires and bring up our water and the way we make up our bread, we have a pan and put the meal in it and stir it up and put it on the fire and when it is done the cook hollows out "come to cooley" and we all gather around and eat very hearty. We have plenty to eat, such as strong vitals. We have flour, meal, beef & pickle pork. We can get vegetables. What have you all done with them Yankees that was in Macon County.

I will tell you that we are the best drilled company in the regiment, we drill 5 hours every day but Sunday. We have battilion drill in the evening.

Charlton, Shell & Stuart all send their respects.

Give my respects to Miss Mollie, also Mr. & Mrs. Walker.

Your friend untill death,

Charley W. Owen

(Direct your letter in care of Tenn. Vol. 2nd. Regiment, Capt. Tyree)

* * * * *

SUMNER COUNTY

CIVIL WAR LETTERS

PREFACE

W. C. POSTON TO COL. A. R. WYNNE

The following letter is a copy of the original one written by W. C. Poston to Colonel A. R. Wynne, Castalian Springs. The letter is at present owned by his grandson, George Wynne of Castalian Springs, which is about 8 miles east of Gallatin, Tennessee, who lives in the century-old house, built by his grandfather, of oak and ash logs.

Col. A. (Alfred) R. Wynne married Almira Winchester, a daughter of Gen. James Winchester, a Revolutionary soldier, also a soldier in the War of 1812, a close friend of Andrew Jackson. This pioneer family included 14 children. Colonel Wynne planted a hickory tree in his yard on the day of the death of Andrew Jackson, which is still standing in the yard of the home site, at Castalian Springs.

* * * * *

Copied by:
Miss Rubye Dillon,
Gallatin, Tennessee,
October 31, 1938.

* * *

SUMNER COUNTY

CIVIL WAR LETTERS
W. C. POSTON TO COL. A. R. WYNNE

Memphis, Tenn.
June 25, 1866

Hon. A. R. Wynne,
Castalian Springs.

Dear Sir,

In view of all the surroundings we think it important that all of the members elected to the Legislature, who were rejected at the last session, should present themselves on the 4th. inst. in obedience to the Governor's call, to demand admission avowedly for the purpose of voting against the ______ of the constitutional amendments. Especially is this necessary, since the message of the President expressing his disapprobation of these amendments.

Meet us at Nashville on the morning of the 3rd. at 10 O'c.

Yours very Truly,

W. C. Poston

Write to others
in your vicinity.

* * * * *

SUMNER COUNTY

CIVIL WAR RECORD
COMPANY K. SECOND REGIMENT ROLL

The following record was copied from the original paper of Col. A. R. Wynne of Castalian Springs, Tennessee, who had sons enlisted in the Confederate Army. This paper is at present owned by a grandson of Col. Wynne, George Wynne, who lives at the original home of Col. Wynne in the old log house, at Castalian Springs, about 8 miles East of Gallatin, Tennessee.

Copied by Miss Rubye Dillon, Gallatin, Tennessee - November 1, 1938.

Roll of Company K. (Sumner Greys) second Regiment of Tennessee Volunteers, mustered into service of the Confederate States at Lynchburg, Virginia, May 14, 1861.

Officers

Humphrey Bate	Capt.	Rich Wynne	2d. Serg.
Scott Davis,	1st. Lieut.	P. B. Swaney,	3d. Serg.
T. P. Thompson,	2d. Lieut.	P. S. Youree,	4th. Serg.
H. Chenault,	3d. Lieut.	J. W. Roberson,	2d. Cor.
C. B. Rogan,	1st. Serg.	J. Crenshaw,	3rd. Cor.

J. W. Wiseman, 4th. Cor.

Privates

Alexander, Richard
Bate, James H.
Bate, Humphrey H.
Bentley, Andrew J.
Bird, Mathew L.
Boren, James M.
Branham, John T.
Bryson, George G.
Burton, James
Carr, William C.
Cooke, Van B.
Dickerson, Thomas H.
Dickerson, James W.
Drake, Edwin L.
Fergusson, W. W.
Foster, William R.
Thompson, Glenn S.
Hallum, Henry
Hamilton, John L.
Harper, Alfred N.
Haynes, James W.
Head, Milton E.
Hibbitt, John B.
Holt, James A.
Anglea, Durrett B.
Johnson, Stephen C.
Jones, Raymond
Jones, John W.
Kennedy, T. J.
Lewis, James M.
Littleton, William T.
Love, Tilmon C.
Mansker, William T.
Martin, William R.
McDaniel, James R.
Mcgee, Jesse
McKendree, James N.
Padgitt, William D.
Padgitt, William W.
Patterson, Lawson M.
Peddicord, Columbus A.
Pike, John T.
Quinn, William
Rives, Richard B.
Roark, John A.
Rogan, John M.
Rucker, Alexander C.
Sarner, James W.

(Company K. Second Regiment Roll, p. 2)

Hunt, William T.
Hunt, Thomas J.
Jamison, James B.
Shaner, Milton L.
Smith, Wade H.
Staley, David B.
Stone, John W.
Stone, Moses B. H.
Suddarth, James M.
Terry, John H.
Thompson, G. W.
Turner, John B.
Webb, William D.

Saunders, James N.
Scurlock, Robert F.
Shelton, Dawson J.
Williams, William D.
Williams, William F.
Wilkes, John T.
Winchester, Napoleon B.
Wright, Robert
Wynne, Joseph G.
Wynne, Andrew J.
Winn, Edmund A.
Young, Elmore A.
Youree, John R.

* * * * *

CIVIL WAR RECORDS
THE UNION SONG

The following record is a copy of the Union Song, which was copied from Circuit Court Execution Docket, 1849 - 1855. It is written in the back of this book, and bears the date of December 18th. 1865.

Copied by Miss Rubye Dillon, Gallatin, Tennessee - November 15, 1938.

THE UNION SONG

Lets sing a song before we part,
A song to cheer us at the start,
Away, Away, Away,
So here's goodby to all the dear
That's left of the Ottawa Volunteers,
And Away, Away, Away.

Chorus

We are fighting for the Union, hurrah, hurrah,
With many a whack we'll clear the track,
And send the Rebels a howling back,
Away, Away, for we'r for the Union.

The North is starting up at last,
And men are gathering thick and fast,
Away, Away, Away,
For we are for the Union,
The Quaker States are pouring in New York.

* * * * *

Dec. 18th. 1865.

CIVIL WAR LETTER
TO COLONEL A. R. WYNNE

The following letter is a copy of the original one written to Col. A. R. Wynne of Castalian Springs, Tennessee, supposedly by one of his sons, whose name is not known by the copyist. The letter is at present time owned by George Wynne, Castalian Springs, about 8 miles East of Gallatin, Tennessee, Sumner County. George Wynne is the grandson of Col. Wynne, and lives in the original old log house.

Copied by Miss Rubye Dillon, Gallatin, Tennessee - November 1, 1938.

Camp Jackson,
June 26th. 1861.

Col. A. R. Wynne,

Dear Sir:

Having neglected to write to you up to this time I feel somewhat ashamed according to my promise to you when we left. However, I do not suppose you would have gained any information by me writing upon the other, no doubt you are in receipt of letters from some that are in our camps that are much better qualified to give you a correct report of things in general than I have. In fact it is impossible to come to any correct conclusion in regards to the movements of the two armys. It is true that things are developing more than at any former time. Gen. Beauregard is moving his forces on towards Alexandria, he is undoubtedly within cannon shot of Alexandria. He is now throwing up batteries with the intention of commencing a bombardment upon Alexandria in a very few days, so says one report, another rumor is that Gen. Beauregard is not to make an attack upon Alexandria untill after the meeting of the Federal Congress and that a proposition for an adjustment of the difficulties will be made.

Gen. Holmes, our Briga. Gen. has written to Gen. Lee to have us sent to hanassa junction so that we may have a chance to be in the fight at Alexandria & Washington City.

I suppose you think we will run again as you say we did at Aquio Creek. You have not as much confidence in us as the Virginians have. They believe we can whip Lincoln's whole army. I must admit that I am astonished and supprised at Virginians ever being called brave men, beyond a doubt in my mind they have not the pluck to stand and meet the enemy face to face.

Gen. Beauregard has under his command at hanassas Junction upwards of thirty thousand troops, and by every train they bring more, making an average of one thousand each day, he wants forty thousand troops to carry out his object in attacking Alexandria and Washington City.

Everything is perfectly quiet at Aqua Creek. The Pawnee & Freeborn war steamers are still lying off in sight of our Batteries. There are also about eighteen or twenty tug boats lying off with them. We do not apprehend any great damage from this great point. I think they are satisfied with us there. They will occasionally slip up on us and fire two or three _____ and then run off out of rainge of our guns.

We arrest spys every day, they tell us no evidence at all. Every one is ready and willing to do some tall fighting for the South. We ______ one he made a proposal to go in bathing in the Potomac, and the first thing every one knew he was a half a mile from the bank, making his way to the Pawnee, he was shot at some twenty times, but was not hit by any of them.

The boys are getting along tolerably well.

We are having - - - (The rest of the letter is missing)

* * * * *

SUMNER COUNTY

RESOLUTION ON DEATH OF HENRY CLAY HERMANS

The following is a copy of a resolution in the possession of Miss Annie Brown, North Water Street, Sumner County, Gallatin, Tenn.

Copied by Mrs. Alice Baker Guthrie, Gallatin, Tennessee - Oct. 15, 1938.

Where as in the great economy of Divine Providence Henry Clay Hermans a much loved member of the Gallatin Sunday school was removed from our midst by sudden death on the 26 of June 1873, That we deeply deplore the loss of our friend and associate yet bow submissively to the will of our Creator, who doth all things well.

Resolved that we tender our deepest sympathies to his parents and relatives and implore the God we serve to bestow on them a large measure of his consoling grace and enable them to say the Lord gave, the Lord hath taken away, Blessed be the name of the Lord.

Resolved that a copy of these resolutions be furnished the bereaved family of the deceased and published in the Nashville Christian Advocate.

G. S. Jackson
Mrs. Carrie Wright
R. Beebee

Aug. 3, 1873 Gallatin

SUMNER COUNTY

INVITATION

The following is a copy of an invitation in Mrs. Walter Love's possessions. It was sent to her grand mother.

Copied by Mrs. Alice Baker Guthrie, Gallatin, Tennessee - Oct. 15, 1938

INVITATION TO BALL

The company of Miss Sallie Franklin is solicited at a ball to be held at Wm. Triggś in the town of Gallatin on the fourth day of July next to commence at four oclock p.m.

Managers

Alfred H. Douglass
John H. Bowen
Robert M. Boyers
William Hadley

June 13, 1816

SUMNER COUNTY

INVITATION

The following is a copy of an invitation belonging to George Wynne, who lives at Castalian Springs, about 8 miles east of Gallatin, Sumner County, Tennessee.

Copied by Miss Rubye Dillon, Gallatin, Tennessee - October 31, 1938.

ODD FELLOWS' BALL

The pleasure of your company is solicited at a Ball to be given at the Odd Fellows in Nashville, at their new Hall, on Thursday the 11th of October 1849.

T. T. Smiley	Wm. A. Cheatham
E. A. Raworth	I. M. Jones
Geo. W. Owen	Wm. S. Howard
R. N. Williams	G. W. Cunningham
M. S. P. Hensley	Wm. C. McMurry
Jos. Edwards	Jos. G. Brown

A. M. McKenzie Master of Ceremonies

SUMNER COUNTY

INVITATION

The following is a copy of an invitation belonging to George Wynne of Castalian Springs, about 8 miles east of Gallatin, Sumner County, Tennessee.

Copied by Miss Rubye Dillon, Gallatin, Tennessee - October 31, 1938.

COMMENCEMENT PARTY

You are respectfully invited to attend a commencement party at Baird's Hotel, Lebanon on the 23d of June 1857 at 8 o'clock P.M.

Managers

John B. Walton	Jas. T. Lockridge
H. E. Topp	John C. Carter
W. D. Jocoway	Hugh P. Bone
D. M. Wisdom	Jno. M. Burke, Jr.
L. Houck	A. J. Burton
J. B. Peyton	W. H. Foster
H. H. Bedford	F. Valyent
J. H. Hicks	J. W. Messenger
W. P. Mills	Robert J. Bowen

SUMNER COUNTY BIBLE, FAMILY AND TOMBSTONE RECORDS

At the property of Dimp Briley, Highway 109 in Portland, there is a grave of Shanley McCloud, b. March 31, 1885, d. March 5, 1898. There are other graves there, but they do not have tombstones.
Susan Nancy Briley (Summers) is buried there.

Information from Glenn Summers
1212 Bell Grimes Road
Nashville, TN 37207

183

www.ingramcontent.com/pod-product-compliance
Lightning Source LLC
Chambersburg PA
CBHW080239270326
41926CB00020B/4298
9780788487705